600 FESTIVALS RIGHT IN YOUR OWN BACKYARD™

festivals.com®

Cover and text design by Beth Farrell
Text production by Sheila Hackler
Production assistance by Kylee Krida

Front cover illustration by Beata Szpura/Illustration Works

ISBN: 1-58619-044-X
Library of Congress Control Number: 2003102749

First Printing
April 2003
Printed in Canada

Published by Community Events Publishing
in collaboration with

Festivals.com
Seattle, Washington
http://festivals.com

ELTON-WOLF PUBLISHING

Elton-Wolf Publishing
Seattle, Washington
www.elton-wolf.com

Acknowledgments

Thanks to all of the people who contributed, helped and encouraged the venture that has resulted in this book: First, to my wife Jane. Without her constant support and encouragement, none of this Internet and publishing adventure would be possible. Next, to Beth Farrell, president of Elton-Wolf Publishing, and her team: Hazel Cox, Sheila Hackler, Kylee Krida and Elton Welke; to Dave DeWitt, Sarah O'Hanlon, Jane Holman, Joe Austin, Patrick Burns, Beverly Kantrowitz, Hannah Wiley, Janet Kersey, Judy Lynn, Estela Dorn, Cathy Walters, Shelley Calkins, Janet Wilhelm, Dick Nicholls, Sandra Dartus, Terry Andrye, James Dick, Roberta Healey, Ed Mendoza, Anne Gremillion, Isaac Malkin, Kim Billiard, Bill Clarke, Mary Burdette, Kim Peterson, Tina Brace, April Tunnell, Charla Fogle, Ronnie Stewart, Joel Finegold, Wendy Brenner, Laurie McConnell, Tiffanie Zajac, Ed Bautista, and Les Siemans; all of whom were the first to see the value of a national book on community festivals; and to the executive directors, general managers and staffs of the festivals, fairs and community special events that have listed with and continue to update their listings on Festivals.com.

– Jim Shanklin
Festivals.com
Community Events Publishing

Special thanks to Jim Shanklin for creating a brilliant Web site dedicated to facilitating the desire of each of us to have fun in our own backyard.

– Beth Farrell
President and CEO
Elton-Wolf Publishing
Community Events Publishing

Dedicated to the fun-loving spirit in each of us.

600 FESTIVALS

RIGHT IN YOUR OWN BACKYARD

FEATURED FESTIVALS

"The most wasted of all days is one without laughter."

e.e.cummings

Alabama

Mobile International Festival
Mobile, Alabama

Arizona

Cochise Cowboy Poetry and Music Gathering
Sierra Vista, Arizona

California

Santa Maria Elk's Rodeo & Parade
Santa Maria, California

Gilroy Garlic Festival
Gilroy, California

Hayward-Russell City Blues Festival
Oakland, California

San Jose Holiday Parade
San Jose, California

Florida

Biketoberfest
Daytona Beach Florida

Chasco Fiesta
New Port Richey, Florida

Hispanic Heritage Festival
Miami, Florida

Idaho

Boise River Festival
Boise, Idaho

Illinois

Bagelfest
Mattoon, Illinois

Chicago Humanities Festival
Chicago, Illinois

Iowa

Cedar Rapids Freedom Festival
Cedar Rapids, Iowa

Louisiana

French Quarter Festival
New Orleans, Louisiana

Red River Revel Arts Festival
Shreveport, Louisiana

Satchmo Summer Fest
New Orleans, Louisiana

Massachusetts

Revere Beach Seafood Festival
Revere, Massachusetts

Michigan

Muskegon Summer Celebration
Muskegon, Michigan

Missouri

Silver Dollar City
Branson, Missouri

Nevada

Reno Jazz Festival
Reno, Nevada

Tri-County Fair & Stampede
Winnemucca, Nevada

New Jersey

Academy of Music Summer Festival
Mahwah, New Jersey

New Mexico

National Fiery Foods & Barbeque Show
Albuquerque, New Mexico

New York

Chenango Summer MusicFest
Hamilton, New York

Finger Lakes Wine Festival
Watkins Glen, New York

Grey Fox Bluegrass Festival
Ancramdale, New York

Saratoga Festival & Dressage
Saratoga Springs, New York

North Carolina

CulloWHEE! ArtsFest
Cullowhee, North Carolina

Ohio

National Tractor Pulling Championships
Bowling Green, Ohio

Rhode Island

Rhythm & Roots Festival
Charlestown, Rhode Island

Schwepps Great Chowder Cook-off
Newport, Rhode Island

Tennessee

Celebrate Freedom!
Pigeon Forge, Tennessee

Texas

International Festival –
Institute at Round Top
Round Top, Texas

Utah

Utah Arts Festival
Salt Lake City, Utah

Washington/Oregon

Best of the Northwest
Seattle, Washington
Portland, Oregon

UW Summer Arts Festival
Seattle, Washington

Washington State International Kite Festival
Long Beach, Washington

Wisconsin

Warrens Cranberry Festival
Warrens, Wisconsin

Mobile International Festival

Week before Thanksgiving
Arthur R. Outlaw–
Mobile Convention Center
www.mobileinternationalfestival.org
(251) 470-7730
Discounted advance tickets

The Mobile International Festival takes thousands of visitors around the world. The three-day festival of over sixty countries began in 1983 with the purpose of educating citizens about other cultures. Executive Director Estela Dorn said, "The International Festival offers everyone, from school children to adults, the opportunity to know the world. When people understand each other and realize our differences, these barriers can diminish and even be removed."

Each year, festival activities are given a theme which becomes the focus of the cultural booths. Over 1,000 volunteers make the festival a feast for the senses by creating these festive cultural booths displaying posters, dolls, stamps, and handmade goods from their native countries. Other festival members manage the tantalizing food booths, selling authentic dishes and beverages from more than twenty countries. Visitors can sample German pastries, Mexican quesadillas, Philippine adobo, Polish sausage, Japanese sushi, Vietnamese spring rolls, Colombian coffee, Puerto Rican empanadas and many more treats.

In addition to eye-catching displays and tasty treats, the festival boasts lively performances by dancers, clowns, singers, musicians, storytellers, and martial artists. The Mariachi serenades the crowd; Japanese drummers thrill audiences with their precision and rhythm; the Russians strum the balalaikas; and belly dancers delight visitors.

Festival's honors include a Tribute in the US Congressional Record, rated in the "Top 20 Events in the Southeast" twice and nominated "Event of the Year" for three years.

AZ

Photo © 2003 by Siemens Enterprises, Inc. and its licensors

Cochise Cowboy Poetry and Music Gathering

Held annually in early February
Sierra Vista, Arizona
www.cowboypoets.com
(520) 459-3868 or (800) 288-3861

Cowboy poetry and music has been part of the West for over one hundred years. Though it is seldom, if ever, heard in motion pictures about the West, it certainly was a part of the working world of cowboys. Cowboy poetry was born as they attempted to relate their event-filled daily life by the light of an open campfire or gathered around the bunkhouse stove. It is perpetuated today by individuals who still believe in "The Cowboy Way."

The annual Cochise Cowboy Poetry and Music Gathering in Sierra Vista, Arizona, continues the tradition of bringing this true Western art form to today's audience. In its 12th year in 2004, The Gathering has become the Cowboy Poetry and Music event to attend or perform at in the Southwest. It is a premier event featuring three days of performances of more than 50 poets and musicians from around the Western States in a variety of different venues: three stage performances, a day of simultaneous thematic programs, jam sessions and more.

Come join us in Southeast Arizona to enjoy cowboy storytellers, poets, singers and musicians as they give tribute to our Western heritage and ranching in the Southwest. The Gathering is held every year on the first consecutive Friday, Saturday and Sunday of February.

For more information, visit our web site, or contact The Gathering at CCPMG Attn: Info; PO Box 3201; Sierra Vista, AZ 85636-3201.

CA

Santa Maria Elk's Rodeo & Parade

First full weekend of June, Thurs.-Sun.
Elk's/Unocal Event Center
www.elks1538.com
(805) 925-4125

60 years of extravaganza

The Santa Maria Elk's Rodeo & Parade is one of the biggest events held here on the Central Coast every year. Thousands of rodeo fans, both local and "out of towners" bring their families to enjoy all the festivities.

The Elk's Rodeo is a four-day event held at the Elk's /Unocal Event Center. It is always the first full weekend of June, beginning on Thursday evening and ending on Sunday afternoon. The rodeo begins each performance with skydiving and a tribute to our country. During this three hour exciting event you will see the adrenaline-rushing Wild Horse Race, the famous Mutton Bustin', the six PRCA events—which include Bull Riding, Bronc Riding, Calf Roping, Steer Wrestling, Bareback Riding and WPRA Barrel Racing—local team roping, specialty acts and much more. You will also see rodeo's top announcers, bullfighters and stock contractors.

Thursday evening is "Family Night" allowing children 12 years of age and under free admission with an adult ticket purchase. Friday night is the Elk's Rodeo Queen Coronation where a new Elk's Rodeo Queen is crowned. Sunday is our rodeo finals and "Vehicle Giveaway." The Elk's Parade is held on Saturday at 9:00 A.M. and runs south on Broadway from Mill to Stowell. The parade features over 200 entries, including marching bands, majorettes, color guards, floats, equestrians and clowns, and fills the streets with nearly 25,000 viewers.

In conjunction with the Elk's Rodeo & Parade, there are five fun-filled events leading up to rodeo weekend, including the "Elk's Queen Kickoff," introducing the new rodeo queen candidates, the "Rodeo Kickoff & Auction" featuring many donated items, the Beard-A-Reno beard growing contest and party, a western dance and the "Rodeo Banquet." All events include a Santa Maria Style BBQ and live entertainment and are held at the Santa Maria Elk's Lodge #1538.

Gilroy Garlic Festival

July 25, 26, 27, 2003
Gilroy, California
www.gilroygarlicfestival.com
(408)842-1625

A lot can change in 25 years.

Back in 1979, most people had never heard of Gilroy, California. And Garlic was still a somewhat exotic herb used mostly in Italian and Asian cuisine. But then Dr. Rudy Melone, who had recently moved to Gilroy, proposed hosting an annual festival to celebrate the end of the garlic harvest and raise money for local charities. Garlic grower Don Christopher and chef Val Filice thought it was a "crazy idea," but they (along with hundreds of other volunteers) agreed to help. The rest is history. An anticipated first-year attendance of 5,000 jumped to 15,000, and the city of Gilroy and its now-famous Garlic Festival have continued to grow ever since. Though much has changed since 1979, today's Garlic Festival remains true to the vision of its founders. Hosted by over 4,000 volunteers, we proudly offer the same great food and summer family entertainment that have made it one of the premier food festivals in the world. And we have more to offer than ever before.

The world-famous Gourmet Alley, our gigantic outdoor kitchen that is the heart of the festival, where the "Pyro Chefs" cook up garlic-laced calamari and scampi in huge iron skillets over blazing fire pits. And don't forget to try the infamous only-in-Gilroy garlic ice cream! Entertainment includes three stages and several groups of strolling musicians. And on the Cookoff Stage watch cooking demonstrations by celebrity chefs and finalists in our annual recipe contest. Festival souvenirs and unique handmade creations are available in Arts & Crafts areas and Mercantile boutiques. Younger kids can enjoy many different hands-on activities, games, and entertainment and there are fun activities for older kids (and kids-at-heart) too, like rock-climbing walls and the thrilling Got Milk? Extreme Sports Tour. You can even try making your own garlic braid!

Whether you're a "seasoned" veteran or a first-time visitor, we hope you'll come help us celebrate our 25th anniversary at the 2003 Gilroy Garlic Festival!

CA

Hayward-Russell City Blues Festival

July 12–13, 2003
Hayward City Hall Plaza
Oakland, California
www.geocities.com/hipwayblues
(510) 836-2226
Produced by Bay Area Blues Society

Hayward-Russell City Blues Festival has a rich history in the growth of the West Coast Blues style. The Festival commemorates a time when Russell City, within the confines of Hayward, was a little town of African Americans from the Deep South. As a proving ground for many blues legends–artists like Big Joe Turner and Big Mama Thornton who played Texas, Arkansas and Louisiana style blues–Russell City, known for its clubs with dirt floors, bootleg electricity, and a steady stream of musicians is now gone as a separate community, but its legacy lives on.

The Bay Area Blues Society produces this festival, along with seven others in the Bay Area. Its mission is to promote the West Coast Blues sound in northern California through performances and education. In addition to the festivals listed below, the Society produces a weekly blues series in downtown Oakland and an annual West Coast Blues Hall of Fame Awards Show. The Bay Area Blues Society proudly represents and assists the following festivals and events:

- Blues from Around the County & Motown Golden Days Review
- Hayward-Russell City Blues Festival
- Home Grown Blues Series
- The Music They Played on 7th Street Festival
- Oakland Art & Soul Festival
- Siskiyou Blues & Heritage Festival
- Swans Song Blues Series
- Vallejo Blues & Heritage Festival

San Jose Holiday Parade

1st Sunday following Thanksgiving weekend
Step-off at 8:30 A.M.
San José, California
www.sanjoseholidayparade.com
(408) 277-3303
Free Admission
Parking in Downtown San José parking lots
(www.sjdowntownparking.com)

Downtown Holiday Spectacular!

The San Jose Holiday Parade has been recognized for more than 20 years as a downtown holiday spectacular. The international award-winning San Jose Holiday Parade tradition began in 1981 when Santa Claus rode in a horse-drawn carriage to the park for the opening of the Christmas in the Park display at Plaza de Cesar Chavez in Downtown San José and it has become a very important part of the community and businesses. The parade has helped people rediscover the Downtown's museums, restaurants, shops, and activities.

Named one of the "Top 25 Parades in America," 100,000 spectators view specialty units, marching bands, guest celebrities, giant helium balloons, and exciting floats. Each year, numerous floats compete for prestigious awards and top middle school and high school marching bands compete for honors in the Battle of the Bands competition. A sneak preview of the holiday festivities can be seen at the Annual Inflation Celebration held the night before the parade. The festivities include the inflation of giant helium balloons, a preview of parade floats, and performances by specially selected parade units.

After the parade, spectators can enjoy ParadeFest @ Christmas in the Park. ParadeFest includes community entertainment, wellness and community information, the presentation of the Battle of the Bands awards and a holiday concert by the U.S. Marine Corps Band.

Biketoberfest®

October 16–19, 2003
Daytona Beach, Florida
www.biketoberfest.org
(866) 296-8970

Annually, motorcycle enthusiasts and visitors alike from around the world come to the Daytona Beach area to enjoy the fun, friendship and festivities of this autumn motorcycle festival.

Held each October, Biketoberfest® features a variety of activities such as:

- Motorcycle Racing at Daytona International Speedway
- World Famous Main Street & Beach Street rally events and entertainment
- Shopping and food area-wide from unique collector and event items, to turkey legs and fresh seafood
- Charity rides and fundraisers with celebrity participants
- Bike shows of all types for novices or experts alike
- Concerts, swap meets, expo, demo rides and a wide variety of spectator events for all ages

You do not have to be a biker to enjoy Biketoberfest®. Many people attend just to observe the fun, colorful, eclectic collection of bikes and people.

The Daytona Beach area is also home to some of the biggest names in motorcycling including the Daytona International Speedway, Carl's Speed Shop, Corbin Saddles and Arlen Ness that are great locations to visit anytime. Add to that some of the most famous saloons in the world like Boothill, Iron Horse, Broken Spoke, Froggy's, Dirty Harry's, Pub 44, Cabbage Patch and more....

Accommodations during Biketoberfest® are plentiful and range from world-class hotels to superior rated (SSL) small properties.

For more information on Biketoberfest® contact Janet Kersey, CFE, Event Director, Daytona Beach Area Convention & Visitors Bureau, jkersey@daytonabeachcvb.org, 1-800-296-8970 ext. 117.

Chasco Fiesta

March 18–28, 2004
New Port Richey, Florida
www.chascofiesta.com
(727) 842-7651

The first Chasco Fiesta in 1922 was held to raise money for the community library. The Chasco Fiesta, March 18–28, 2004, offers eleven full days of entertainment and activity, ten nights of free music, and a Country Concert featuring national recording stars. No longer a fund-raiser for a local library, Chasco now benefits more than thirty not-for-profit organizations.

Held on the banks of the Pithlachascotee River (the "Cotee") in New Port Richey, the festival allows visitors to witness a traditional Native American Festival. Native American people from as far away as New Mexico and Oklahoma participate in this event, which offers $10,000 in dance prize money.

Other Chasco Fiesta activities include a premier street parade, oldest running boat parade in the state, children's Village, a car & truck show, a baby contest, a river raft race, a three-day flea market & antique show, softball tournament, arts & crafts festival, stamp show, road race, bike tour, in-line skate, golf tournament and of course, a carnival. If all that activity makes you hungry, you'll find food in plentiful quantities and unlimited varieties.

Make your plans now to come enjoy the free entertainment and activities that make up one of Florida's longest running festivals—the 82nd Annual Chasco Fiesta.

Hispanic Heritage Festival

October 1–31, 2003
Miami, Florida
www.hispanicfestival.com
(305) 461-1014

One of the top ten Hispanic Festivals in the United States and among the top forty events in the nation, The Hispanic Heritage Festival attracts over 300,000 people to its month-long celebration of Hispanic culture, traditions and entertainment.

The Festival, now in its 30th year, is the greatest series of cultural and sporting events that celebrate Hispanic Heritage month. Every October, the city of Miami plays host to exciting music and food fairs, award dinners, an art exhibition, a beauty pageant, a national poster competition, an essay competition and more!

The Festival is a unique vehicle for those companies wishing to reach the growing Hispanic market, which has a buying power estimated at $12 million. Blue chip corporations like General Motors, AT&T, BellSouth, Budweiser, American Airlines, and Burger King have found our Festival an ideal tool to reach South Florida's Hispanics.

Boise River Festival

Held annually the last full week of June
404 S. 8th Street, Suite 404
Boise, Idaho
www.boiseriverfestival.org
(208) 338-8887
Free admission

IDAHO
www.visitid.org

ID

Welcome to the Boise River Festival!

This week-long, citywide celebration of music, art and entertainment is held the last full week of June in the beautiful parks of Boise, Idaho.

Along with headliner entertainment, the Festival features a Balloon Rally and evening Night Glow, two parades, eight performance stages, an international World Showcase, a crafts fair and over ninety food vendors. A Fun Run, Hole-in-One contest, oodles of kid's activities, and a Carnival round out the list of "must-do's" for the whole family. The Festival culminates with a Fireworks Spectacular on Sunday night, bringing a dramatic close to the entertainment-packed weekend.

River Festival sponsors enjoy the unique opportunity to reach a growing Northwest market with an aggregate attendance of 500,000. Recognized as one of the "Top 40 Events in the United States" and "Top 10 Summer Festivals in the Country," the River Festival offers quality impressions in an award-winning environment. Companies will join current sponsors and corporate leaders, such as Albertsons, AT&T Wireless, Blue Cross of Idaho, Coca-Cola, Hewlett-Packard, Micron, Miller Brewing, U.S. Bank, Wells Fargo, Wildhorse Resort and Casino, and Star Systems.

Boasting recognition as "America's Finest Family Festival," you will find an entire park dedicated to kids with non-stop children's programming and interactive fun. Before or after the Festival, enjoy the great restaurants, shopping and recreation in downtown and surrounding Boise area.

Experience the Boise River Festival! Join this exciting event as a sponsor, performer, volunteer or as our guest!

Celebrating the Spirit of America
BAGELFEST
Mattoon, Illinois

Mattoon • Illinois
a city for all
S•E•A•S•O•N•S

Bagelfest

Since 1985

Last full weekend in July
July 23–26, 2003
July 28–31, 2004
Mattoon Welcome Center • Peterson House
500 Broadway Avenue • Mattoon, Illinois
www.mattoonillinois.org
(800) 500-6286

IL

Are you passionate about bagels?

Do you anxiously anticipate your next opportunity to savor the flavor of the smooth cream cheese mixing with sweet preserves on top of a mouth watering, perfectly toasted bagel? If so, mark your calendars, load up the family, and make a trip to the Mattoon Bagelfest! We are the only production facility of Lender's Bagels in the nation. This gives us the opportunity to hold a unique festival, which takes place every summer during the last full weekend in July. The World's Biggest Bagel was baked for Bagelfest, weighing in at 563 lbs. and measuring 59 3/16" in diameter and 12 ½" in height according the to Guinness Book of World Records 1997. At the World's Largest Bagel Breakfast, we give away more than 50,000 bagels, cream cheese, honey, butter, and jelly. Our annual celebration also includes a beauty pageant, concerts, a parade, craft and food vendors, contests, races, tournaments, a carnival and more!

Chicago Humanities Festival

October 25 – November 9, 2003
and ongoing year-round
Chicago, Illinois
www.chfestival.org
(312) 661-1028
FREE tickets for students and educators
$5 in advance, $6 at the door

chf
Chicago Humanities festival

A celebration of ideas

For approximately two weeks each fall, Chicago turns into the coolest place on the planet, as a plethora of writers, painters, photographers, performers and thinkers arrive en masse to bewitch and enthrall audiences.

—Julia Keller, Chicago Tribune, December 30, 2001

Held annually during the first two-weeks of November, this festival is staged in collaboration with nearly 35 Chicago cultural and educational institutions. It features over 100 thought-provoking presenters who collectively consider and interpret a central theme. The festival brings the best and brightest scholars, artists, authors, historians, journalists, performers, filmmakers, critics, and personalities from around the world to examine issues through the lens of the humanities. It also includes a popular Children's Humanities Festival.

Year-round programs extend the inquiry into the year's theme through readings, lectures, discussions, screenings, seminars, tours, and performances. Educational workshops and seminars bring the humanities to teachers and students in creative ways.

Past themes include: Crime & Punishment, Birth & Death, Work & Play, Old & New, Words & Pictures, and Brains & Beauty. Individual audience sizes range from 25 to nearly 1,200, with many in the 100-200 range. An estimated 45,000 people attend the Festival each year.

The Chicago Humanities Festival, founded in 1989, is an independent, not-for-profit organization committed to ensuring that the humanities play a rich and vital role in civic life.

Cedar Rapids Freedom Festival

June 26–July 6, 2003
Cedar Rapids, Iowa
www.freedomfestival.com
(319) 365-8313

For good, old-fashioned, patriotic fun where there's something for everyone, plan to celebrate America in the Heartland by attending the Cedar Rapids Freedom Festival from June 26th – July 6th, 2003. A family-oriented festival with over 70 different events, the costs are very affordable and most admissions are FREE with a $2 Freedom Festival button.

Included in the many events are outdoor concerts – rock & roll, symphony pops, jazz and folk; a fireworks competition; an Air Show; a patriotic parade; many fun children's activities; Great Cardboard Boat Regatta; Dragon Boat Races; 8k foot race; museum tours; a Salute to Heroes; a Barbecue Round Up; ice skating; pig roasts and picnics; and THREE nights of the most spectacular fireworks the Midwest has seen, choreographed to fabulous, musical soundtracks.

Jump in your car with the kids and grandparents, drive over to Cedar Rapids, Iowa – in the Heart of the Heartland and only 20 miles from Interstate 80 – to spend a few days at the Cedar Rapids Freedom Festival, presented by Wells Fargo. You'll want to make it an annual family tradition!

We'd love to "bring you home" to celebrate!

French Quarter Festival

April 10–13, 2003
French Quarter • New Orleans, Louisiana
Bourbon St. to the Mississippi River,
Canal St. to Esplanade Ave.
www.fqfi.com
(504) 522-5730

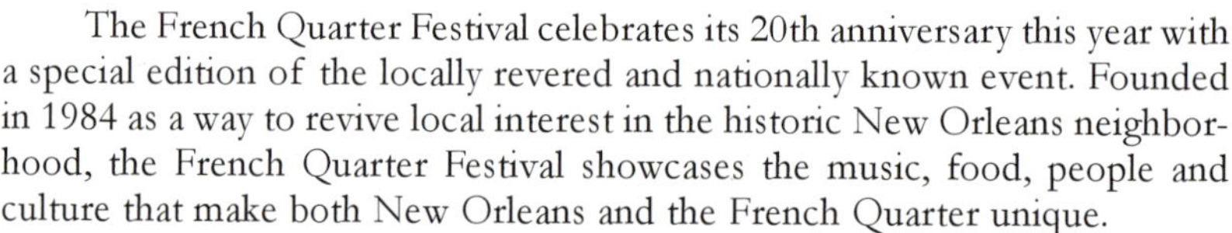

The French Quarter Festival celebrates its 20th anniversary this year with a special edition of the locally revered and nationally known event. Founded in 1984 as a way to revive local interest in the historic New Orleans neighborhood, the French Quarter Festival showcases the music, food, people and culture that make both New Orleans and the French Quarter unique.

The three-day celebration, held annually in April, boasts the claim of being Louisiana's largest free annual music festival. Festivities include a second-line parade, 5K race, a "Guess the Weight of the World's Largest Praline" contest, children's activities, historic courtyard tours and more. However, the festival's signature draws are its music and food. This year, 300,000 festival-goers are expected to enjoy over 100 hours of live music on 15 stages throughout the French Quarter and along the Mississippi River. Nearly 1500 renowned local musicians are featured in free outdoor concerts, performing in every genre from jazz and rhythm & blues to Cajun and zydeco. And the "World's Largest Jazz Brunch" is a highlight for food aficionados, with over 60 food booths serving authentic New Orleans cuisine.

The festival prides itself on its family-friendly atmosphere and is consistently chosen by readers of local publications such as OffBeat Magazine and Gambit Weekly as one of the top three local music festivals. Aided by nearly 1000 volunteers, the French Quarter Festival is truly a community event and, in its 20th year, continues to enjoy widespread local support and national recognition.

Red River Revel Arts Festival

October 4–11, 2003
Shreveport, Louisiana
www.redriverrevel.com
(318) 424-4000

This 8-day celebration of the arts brings the finest in visual and performing arts to the Shreveport riverfront every year. And don't forget the food–26 booths to be exact!

Whether you're out to shop, or just to enjoy the view, you'll be impressed by the variety of quality art–from oil paintings to jewelry, pottery to sculptures–brought to The Revel by more than 100 visual artists from across the country.

Headline entertainers, as well as all the local favorites, perform live each year on our four outdoor stages. Check out our Web site (www.redriverrevel.com) to see who's slated for Revel.03.

Kids build and create their own works of art in an area exclusively designed for them! Arts education for children has always been the center of The Revel. The children's area also brings street performers, parades and world-renowned children's entertainers to keep the kids busy and excited.

This year, The Revel is sponsored by: AllTel, Christus Schumpert, AmSouth Bank, PepsiAmericas, Junior League of Shreveport-Bossier, Inc. and The City of Shreveport.

The Revel draws more than 180,000 people from a five-state region. And it's been around for 27 years!

Satchmo SummerFest

July 31–August 4, 2003
Louisiana State Museum's
Old U.S. Mint (and various
locations citywide)
400 Esplanade Avenue
New Orleans, Louisiana
www.fqfi.org
(504) 522-5730

Discover *What a Wonderful World* you'll find at Satchmo SummerFest – New Orleans' newest festival favorite – a unique, annual birthday salute to native son Louis "Satchmo" Armstrong. Armstrong's musical legacy and cultural contributions have long been praised internationally, and Satchmo SummerFest celebrates the Satchmo spirit with the only annual Armstrong festival held in the United States. The multiple-day event surrounds the weekend of Armstrong's real birthday of August 4 with a whirlwind of festivities. (For years, it was thought that his birthday was on July 4th, until a jazz scholar recently discovered Armstrong's birth certificate.)

The third annual free festival includes centerpiece activities scheduled for July 31–August 4, 2003. From educational and entertaining seminars by jazz enthusiasts and Armstrong colleagues, to free modern and traditional jazz concerts on multiple outdoor stages, Satchmo SummerFest is the type of lively birthday party that only New Orleans can arrange.

Taking place in the world-famous French Quarter and various other locations throughout New Orleans, Satchmo SummerFest is the ultimate tribute to the "International Ambassador of Jazz," in the birthplace of jazz. Originally designed as a one-time tribute for Armstrong's centennial birthday in 2001, the event's success prompted organizers to make it an annual event. Make plans now to enjoy everything Satchmo SummerFest 2003 has to offer—plenty of great music, edu-taining sessions, delicious Crescent City cuisine, colorful art exhibits, a Satchmo Club Strut, hands-on children's activities, a rousing Jazz Mass, authentic second-line street parade and much more jazz-filled summertime fun.

Revere Beach Seafood Festival™

August 9 & 10, 2003–The Second Annual!
Revere, Massachusetts
Revere Beach Boulevard at Beach Street
www.rbsff.com
(508) 788-0333
Free Admission

It's a Feast at the Beach™!

The Revere Beach Seafood Festival™ steams into town for a second great year. To the best from 2002 we've added cool new activities!

- Wide Variety of Seafood and Non-Seafood Items
- Great Bands and DJs
- Giant Classic Car Show – Sunday
- Miss Revere Beach Competition! – Saturday
- Arts and Crafts Vendors
- Historic Swimsuit Show
- Kite Flying
- A No-Alcohol Event
- Right at the Beach! Bring Your Swimsuit!

REVERE BEACH SEAFOOD FESTIVAL™ AUG 9-10, 2003

For attendees, vendors, and corporate exhibitors alike, many key elements help the Festival cook. The Revere Beach Seafood Festival is on track to become one of the largest annual public events in New England. Total attendance may exceed 60,000. The festival is just minutes from Downtown Boston by car or cab, and great public transportation access is provided by the MBTA Blue Line.

A Major Media Promotion is in development, similar to 2002, see our Web site at www.rbsff.com for the 2002 Media Wrap Up. The Revere Beach Seafood Festival supports The Partnership for Revere Beach and the Revere Department of Recreation. The festival itself is supported by The City of Revere and The Metropolitan District Commission.

Muskegon Summer Celebration

June 26–July 6, 2003
Heritage Landing • Muskegon, Michigan
www.summercelebration.com
(231) 722-6250

Summer fun abounds

Looking for summer fun…? Muskegon Summer Celebration is a ten-day, eleven-night festival that has it all. The Celebration is held along the Muskegon Lake waterfront at Heritage Landing in downtown Muskegon, Michigan, just miles from eastern shore of Lake Michigan. Muskegon Summer Celebration is Michigan's largest, and one of the Midwest's premier, music festivals. Great music sets the mood with national recording artists on the Chrysler/Jeep/Dodge Main Stage, and local and regional acts on the Regional Showcase Stage and during Art in the Park at Hackley Park. Over 300 artisans from around the United States join us for the award-winning, juried fine art/craft show, Art in the Park, and the Village Craft Market. Plus, an exciting midway—providing thrills for all ages—and two fireworks displays to dazzle your senses.

The first Saturday features the Art Van Grand Parade, with marching bands, dancers, floats, clowns and much more. Free family fun follows at the Street Fair along Western Avenue, filled with live music, dancing, food, and fun for the entire family. The Depot Expo also provides fun for all throughout the festival. Or, how about joining us for the Plumbs Community Picnic? There's lots of incredible, inexpensive food and fantastic free entertainment and activities to keep everyone occupied. Children's activities throughout the festival keep everyone focused on fun.

Silver Dollar City

399 Indian Point Rd • Branson, Missouri
www.silverdollarcity.com
(800) 831-4FUN

Silver Dollar City, an authentic 1880s theme park and winner of the prestigious Applause Award, the theme park industry's top award of excellence, features more than 100 resident craftsmen, world-class entertainment and attractions, plus four fabulous festivals offering additional fun and excitement April through December.

Each spring America's Largest International Festival, **World-Fest** (April–May), spans the borders and oceans and links people and nations together as hundreds of performers gather at Silver Dollar City to share their culture through the imagery of song, dance and storytelling.

Round up your crew for a summertime adventure as Silver Dollar City lets down any air of well-mannered sophistication and opts for a feast of fun during the **National Kids' Fest** (June–August). From interactive shows and hands on activities to the thrill of 12 exciting rides and attractions, America's Largest Children's Festival is a summer celebration of family fun.

When autumn air is fresh and clear, bring your family together at the **Festival of American Music & Craftsmanship** (September–October), the only place to see, hear and touch the very best of America. Weaving together the finest in crafts and music, the heart and soul of Silver Dollar City festivals honors the voices and hands that fashioned our heritage.

Gather your family together for the most magical time of year as Silver Dollar City celebrates **An Old Time Christmas** (November– December)! Holiday cheer abounds as the City features over four million lights, a spectacular Five-Story Special Effects Christmas Tree, the Holiday Light Parade, plus fabulous production shows and shopping around every corner.

2003 Reno Jazz Festival

CJ Walters, Director
May 1–3, 2003
University of Nevada, Reno
College of Extended Studies/048
www.dce.unr.edu/jazz
(775) 784-4046

The University of Nevada, Reno, is proud to present the 41st annual Reno Jazz Festival. The event is one of the most popular of its kind in the nation, bringing together some of the best and brightest young talent in the country and some of the finest guest clinicians in the world. Instrumental/vocal competitions and clinics are held all day Friday and Saturday, featuring outstanding young jazz performers and world-class clinicians.

The Reno Jazz Festival is produced by the University of Nevada, Reno Department of Music and the College of Extended Studies, with sponsorship from Premier Percussion USA, Sabian, Maytan Music Center, the Nevada Arts Council, and many others.

This year's guest artists include saxophonist Ravi Coltrane, appearing with the University of Nevada, Reno's own faculty jazz group, The Collective, and the Dave Holland Quintet, voted Down Beat's "No. 1 Acoustic Jazz Group of the Year, 2001," and J.J.A.'s "Best Small Ensemble" and "Album of the Year, 2000."

Events

- Ravi Coltrane and The Collective • Nightingale Concert Hall
- Festival Competition and Workshops/Clinics • University of Nevada, Reno Campus
- Dave Holland Quintet, also featuring UNR Jazz Lab I • Lawlor Events Center
- Festival Showcase and Festival Awards Ceremony • Lawlor Events Center

Photo credit: Jess W. Smith

Labor Day Weekend
Winnemucca Events Complex
Winnemucca, Nevada
www.winnemucca.nv.us
(800) 962-2638

Labor Day weekend offers something for everyone!

Whether you enjoy a wild broncin' rodeo, contests, street dances, exhibits, the Buckaroo Hall of Fame, parades, Ronald McDonald, a petting farm or demolition derby you will find entertainment for all ages. Other events that occur throughout the year:

Ranch Hand Rodeo – watch as ranch hands from the area compete in such events as ridin' saddle broncs and milkin' wild cows.

Shooting the West Photography Symposium – enjoy an array of guest speakers, a jam session and have your portfolio critiqued.

Run-a-Mucca Motorcycle Rally – Vrooooom into our biker friendly town over Memorial Day weekend and see the one and only "Burning Bike". Enjoy free concerts, poker runs, a celebrity ride, games, memorial service and a show and shine.

Pair-mutuel Races & Mule Show – the only sanctioned mule event in Nevada, so come on and place a bet on your lucky mule.

Basque Festival - come experience a unique heritage by enjoying Basque cuisine, dancing, parades and games of strength and endurance.

Fifties Fever Car Show & Good Times Street Drags – bring your bobby socks and poodle skirts and treasure a weekend filled with concerts, street dances, parades, poker runs, and the ever-popular show 'n shine of hundreds of classic autos that make nostalgia buffs twist and shout! Don't forget to join one of the few drag races in the world that still takes place (legally) on a public road.

Photo credit:
Kathleen A. Phillips

NJ

The Academy of Music Summer Festival

Isaac Malkin, Artistic Director
June 30–August 3, 2003
Ramapo College • Mahwah, New Jersey
aomfestival@cs.com
(845) 358-7446

The Academy of Music Festival brings to the community a truly international event in which world-renowned artists along with rising young talents will perform in the Sharp Theater at the Berrie Center for the Performing Arts. This event takes place on the beautiful campus of Ramapo College of New Jersey in the idyllic setting of the foothills of the Ramapo Mountains, only 45 minutes from New York City. Among the internationally recognized artists participating in an exciting variety of recitals and chamber music concerts are Boris Belkin, Emanuel Borok, David Geber, Misha Keylin, Mikhail Kopelman, Julia Lichten, and Bracha Malkin.

The Festival also offers a five-week course for gifted young musicians, providing rich experience in solo and chamber music performances for talented string players. The program includes private lessons, chamber music, and master classes, and numerous performing opportunities. It offers a stimulating and challenging curriculum under the guidance of an outstanding faculty. Advanced students will collaborate with faculty and guest artists in chamber music coaching and performances.

The Summer Music Festival culminates with a variety of performances, the highlight of which is the annual Gala Concert, including guest appearances by world-class artists along with outstanding young performers.

Crazy Mary and The Gecko clown around to promote their hot & spicy products.

National Fiery Foods & Barbecue Show

16th Annual in Albuquerque, New Mexico
March 5–7, 2004
Albuquerque Convention Center
www.fiery-foods.com/ffshow
(505) 873-8680
$8 general admission. Children 12 & under free

1st Annual in Houston, Texas
August 1–3, 2003
Reliant Center

The Hottest Shows on Earth!

The main attractions at the shows are the largest collections of hot and spicy products ever assembled in the U.S. There is an astonishing variety of fiery-foods on display, including hot sauces, salsas, barbecue sauces, candies, honeys, chips, pestos, nuts, jams, jellies, snacks, soups, salad dressings, mustards, beans, ketchup and many more. Additionally, some exhibitors offer numerous related, non-food products, including clothing, books, posters, calendars, original art and kitchenware.

Cooking Demonstrations: Dave DeWitt, the "Pope of Peppers," and top chefs will be cooking with fire and smoke! Meet the chefs, sample the dishes, and take home their secrets to haute and hot cuisine.

More than 12,000 people attended the 15th Annual National Fiery-Foods & Barbecue Show—Albuquerque. Join us for a really hot time!

Chenango Summer MusicFest

Held annually the third week in June
Colgate University
13 Oak Drive • Hamilton , New York
http: groups.colgate.edu/musicfest
(315) 228-7642

The Chenango Summer MusicFest is a four-day event annually covering the third weekend in June. It blends chamber music performances, children's concerts, vocal ensemble performances, and jazz and world music concerts with instrument demonstrations, master classes, and other opportunities to mingle closely with the world-class artists involved, such as at an ice cream social and chicken barbeque on the Village Green, a thematic opening night dinner that ties into the concert theme, a wine-tasting featuring regional New York State vintners, or at a competition where area restaurants showcase their specialty desserts. The "feel" of the festival is light and friendly, as well as accessible, and this well-run, high-quality chamber music festival was featured in the April 2001 issue of *Chamber Music America*. Ticket prices are reasonable, with senior citizen and student discounts, as well as advance purchase ticket packages. Most events on the Saturday of the Festival are free. It is the type of festival which music lovers and families will want to visit again and again.

Hamilton is a rural village in the heart of the central NY antiquing district with an award-winning golf course, lovely old architecture and small unique shops. Many Bed and Breakfast accommodations grace the area, complimented by a wide variety of restaurants.

Finger Lakes Wine Festival

Finger Lakes Wine Festival

Held annually in July
July 18–20, 2003
Watkins Glen International
2790 County Route 16 • Watkins Glen, New York
www.FLWineFest.com
(607) 535-2481
Advance sale discounts available
Supported by The Corning Museum of Glass

Celebrate the Taste of the Lakes!

The Finger Lakes Wine Festival brings a break in the racing action at Watkins Glen International for the region's largest wine celebration. Over sixty prestigious wineries from throughout New York will be on hand offering tastings, sales, and wine specials. Enjoy arts and crafts vendors, wine seminars, cooking demonstrations, live jazz and blues, a gourmet food court, pace car rides (hey, it's still The Glen), the Corning Museum of Glass Hot Glass Road Show and much more.

Don't miss our kick-off celebration on Friday night—Launch of the Lakes. There'll be wine, music, hors d'oeuvres...and togas! Come see who will be crowned as this year's King and Queen of the Festival. Wear a toga and it could be you!

Other special events include a champagne breakfast and a gourmet taster's dinner in the track's exclusive Glen Club. Great group event with special pricing available ~ Plenty of free parking ~ Handicap accessible ~ On-site camping ~ Most major activities under cover.

Directions: From Route 17/186 – take Route 14 north or from NYS Thruway (Route 90), take Route 14 south. From Route 14, take Route 414 South. Turn right on County Route 16 at the next stoplight. The track is about 3 miles on the left. Use the Main Gate, and follow event-parking signs.

NY

Photo credit: Dan Dennis

Grey Fox Bluegrass Festival

July 17–20, 2003
Ancramdale, New York
www.GreyFoxBluegrass.com
(888) 946-8495

Each year during the third weekend of July, bluegrass enthusiasts from far and wide gather at the picturesque Rothvoss Farm on the NY-MA-CT border for a weekend of bluegrass bliss known as the Grey Fox Bluegrass Festival. Renown for its award-winning lineup, breathtaking setting, round-the-clock picking, impeccable organization and friendly staff, Grey Fox ranks #1 among thousands of bluegrass fans.

With several performance stages and learning programs, Grey Fox has something for the whole family. The legendary Main Stage delivers four days of the nation's top bluegrass and acoustic artists. Around the grounds, fans can enjoy intimate mini-concerts at the Masters Workshop Stage, kick up their heels at the Dance Pavilion, and be mesmerized by clowns, magicians and storytellers at the Family Stage, where a Ringling Brothers clown even teaches an annual crop of young 'clownees' his tricks of the trade!

For budding musicians, Grey Fox also offers daily hands-on learning sessions and slow jams for adults at the Grass Roots Tent and an intensive four-day Bluegrass Academy for Kids.

NY

Saratoga Festival & Dressage

May 24–26, 2003
Union Avenue Race Course
www.saratogaarcfestival.org

(518) 587-0723
Sponsored by Saratoga County ARC
FEES: $6.00 for adults, $5.00 for groups over 20,
$4.00 for kids 5–12, Free for kids under 5

The 14th Annual Saratoga Festival & Dressage will be held Memorial Day Weekend, from 9:00A.M.–6:00P.M., at the historic Race Course in Saratoga Springs. Hailed as one of the "Top Five Events in NYS" (NYS Department of Economic Development), one of the "Top Hundred Events in North America" (American Bus Association) and "#1 out of 12 Events to visit during the Memorial Day Weekend" (Boston Globe), this activity-filled weekend is packed with entertainment for the entire family and the perfect venue for tour groups.

Over 37,000 people come to enjoy the pageantry of Dressage, 200+ craft and trade exhibitors, an International all-breed show, horse training, Special Olympics riding, carriages, performers in costumes, masters dog agility and frisbee competitions, llamas and alpacas, talent stage, children's activities, antique cars and much more. New in '03–AARP the Magazine Road Show.

Saratoga Springs is the home of the National Museum of Horse Racing and the National Museum of Dance and has been honored with the Great American Place Award and the Great American Main Street Award.

The Event benefits the Saratoga County Association for Retarded Citizens (ARC). This non-profit organization provides a wide variety of services to over 650 individuals with developmental disabilities and their families.

CulloWHEE! ArtsFest

June 20–21, 2003
Western Carolina University
Cullowhee, North Carolina
www.cullowheeartsfest.com
(866) WCU-FEST

The second annual CulloWHEE! ArtsFest at Western Carolina University, a celebration of the fine and performing arts, is scheduled for Friday, June 20, and Saturday, June 21, with two days of live jazz, blues and adult contemporary music featuring national recording artists to be announced at a later date. Festival organizers are promising acts of the same quality as the headliners who performed at the inaugural CulloWHEE! ArtsFest in June 2002—The Manhattan Transfer, David Sanborn, Joe Sample and Bio Ritmo.

The outdoor festival is held on the campus of Western Carolina University in Cullowhee, N.C., located in a scenic valley between the Blue Ridge and Great Smoky Mountains. In addition to performances by musical acts from across the country on two separate stages, the event also will feature fine art on exhibit and for sale. For more information, call WCU's Ramsey Center toll-free at 866-WCU FEST (928-3378), or see our Web site, www.cullowheeartsfest.com.

The National Tractor Pulling Championships

Held annually the third weekend in August
Wood County Fairgrounds
Bowling Green, Ohio
www.pulltown.com
(888) 385-7855

The National Tractor Pulling Championships are held the third weekend in August each year at the Wood County Fairgrounds in Bowling Green, Ohio. The largest attended event of its venue, this championship truck and tractor pull boasts five sessions over a three-day period. These are not your everyday farming and trucking implements. Think of them as trucks and tractors on steroids. Competing divisions include 2- and 4-wheel drive trucks, pro stock, super stock, and super farm tractors, super semi trucks, and mini, limited and unlimited modified tractors all competing for cash and contingency prizes. Also on the grounds are a toy and trade show, sponsor exhibits, retired tractor museum, concessions, souvenir merchandise and an open paddock area to get up close to vehicles and competitors.

Photo credit: Hank Randall

Rhythm & Roots Festival

August 29–31, 2003
Ninigret Park • Charlestown, Rhode Island
www.RhythmAndRoots.com
(888) 855-6940

America's exciting roots music and rhythmic dance styles are what this red-hot Labor Day Weekend festival is all about. Cajun, Zydeco, Swing, Bluegrass, Blues and Tex-Mex take to the Main Stage while dance enthusiasts from up and down the eastern seaboard keep its huge dance floor in motion all weekend.

Over at the Dance Pavilion, patrons learn swing, Cajun and Zydeco dance moves by day to live bands, while nightly Fais Do Dos keep the party going into the wee hours. Meanwhile, the intimate, relaxed atmosphere of the Workshop Tent is the perfect setting for performers to talk about their music and play requests for their appreciative audience.

Children are a very important part of Rhythm & Roots. The Family Stage offers storytelling, puppet shows, concerts and activities such as instrument and mask making workshops, and a Kids' Mardi Gras Parade that winds through the crowd each afternoon.

And there's yet another component to Rhythm & Roots – the irresistible food – every bit as savory as the music! Rhythm & Roots serves up heaps of ethnic and regional dishes – from jambalaya and BBQ to lobster bisque and key lime pie!

On-site camping, unique vendors, bike trails, tennis courts, and freshwater swimming pond. Beaches and oceanfront accommodations are just minutes away. All this on Rhode Island's beautiful south shore!

22nd Annual Schweppes Great Chowder Cook-Off

Saturday, June 7, 2003
Saturday, June 5, 2004

22nd Annual Schweppes Great Chowder Cook-Off

Produced by Newport Waterfront Festivals
at the Newport Yachting Center
Newport, Rhode Island
www.newportfestivals.com
(401) 846-1600

For over two decades, the Schweppes Great Chowder Cook- Off in Newport, Rhode Island has enticed local and regional restaurants and caterers to compete for the title of "Best Chowder in the Nation." The restaurants compete for over $4000 in prizes by entering their specialty chowders in one of three categories– best clam, seafood or creative chowder!

In addition to delicious chowder served by over 30 restaurants, the event also features the "Clam Shack" where restaurants vie for the Best Clam Cakes! Over 50 vendor booths feature marketplace, craft and specialty items for sale.

While enjoying chowder and other delicious cuisine indigenous to Rhode Island, attendees enjoy three stages of music featuring big band, jazz, calypso and rhythm and blues! Highlights also include culinary demonstrations, an extensive children's area with a climbing wall, clowns and other amusements, a silent auction and a community tent.

In addition to the Great Chowder Cook-Off, Newport Waterfront Festivals also produces the Taste of Rhode Island, Newport Waterfront Irish Festival, International Oktoberfest and Sunset Music Festival.

The festivals take place along picturesque Newport Harbor at the Newport Yachting Center on Americas Cup Avenue in historic downtown Newport. For more information call (401) 846-1600 or visit us on line at newportfestivals.com.

August 9–23, 2003
Pigeon Forge, Tennessee
www.mypigeonforge.com
(800) 365-6993

Mark your calendars now for the fourth annual **Celebrate Freedom!** ™ in Pigeon Forge, Tennessee. This outstanding event is filled with special activities designed to honor America's heroes.

Celebrate Freedom!™ recently received the Grand Pinnacle Award from the International Festivals & Events Association, and, it is expected to become one of the most popular events in Pigeon Forge history.

The fourth annual **Celebrate Freedom!™** is scheduled for Aug. 9-23, 2003 and a variety of activities will take place throughout this East Tennessee city during the 15-day salute, including:

- **"Celebrate Freedom! The Musical"**–A musical journey celebrating America's Patriots.
- **Firefighter and Police Challenges**–Individual Police and Firefighter challenges will take place in Patriot Park on Thursday, August 21, 2003.
- **Freedom Forums**–A series of appearances and presentations featuring notable veterans and historians.
- **Canteen Dances**–Featuring Big Band orchestras.
- **Journey to Freedom: War Stories**–Open microphone sessions for veterans to share their personal experiences.

Most Celebrate Freedom! activities are offered free of charge. As an added benefit, veterans, active military personnel, homeland security personnel, EMS, police and firefighters presenting proof of service at Celebrate Freedom Headquarters will receive a special Celebrate Freedom VIP booklet, good for discounts at businesses throughout the city during the 15-day event. Our nation's heroes are always regarded highly in Pigeon Forge, but this VIP booklet is just another way of saying thank you during Celebrate Freedom!

The International Festival–Institute at Round Top

June 1–July 12, 2003
Festival Hill in Round Top, Texas
State Highway 237 at Jaster Road
www.festivalhill.org
(979) 249-3129

THE INTERNATIONAL FESTIVAL-INSTITUTE AT ROUND TOP

TX

The International Festival–Institute at Round Top, founded by internationally acclaimed concert pianist James Dick in 1971, is an intensive six-week summer program for advanced orchestra and chamber music study and performance. From the beginning of June to mid-July each summer, talented young musicians from colleges and conservatories around the world perform concerts, attend master classes and study privately with nationally and internationally-renowned teachers, performers and conductors in the idyllic surroundings of rural central Texas. The 200-acre Festival-Institute campus on Festival Hill in Round Top, population 77, includes a collection of restored 19th century homes, the 1883 Edythe Bates Old Chapel, the magnificent 1100 seat Festival Concert Hall as well as extensive herb and flower gardens, lakes, footpaths, forests and meadowland.

In addition to the six-week summer festival, concerts, forums, lectures and seminars are presented throughout the year on subjects as diverse as gardening, theatre, literature, poetry, art and architecture during the "August-to-April" Series. Festival Hill is also home to extensive collections of music, art, architecture, decorative arts, rare books, manuscripts and antiques. Accommodations on the Festival-Institute campus are available during the "August-to-April" Series and music lovers delight in weekends spent on Festival Hill in either the historic 1902 Menke House or beautiful studio rooms. Dedicated to promoting the fine arts and humanities as integral to one's cultural life, The Festival-Institute's world-class performances of music and numerous other forms of creative expression year-round provide a necessary and vital public service to the people of Texas, the nation and the world in a rare place where beauty and truth are celebrated and everyone is welcome.

Utah Arts Festival

June 19–22, 2003
Salt Lake City, Utah
www.uaf.org
(801) 322-2428

The mission of the Utah Arts Festival Foundation, Inc. is to produce the annual Utah Arts Festival for the purpose of promoting the arts and enhancing the quality of life in Utah.

UT

The Utah Arts Festival strives to maintain the highest artistic quality and excellence.

The Utah Arts Festival presents a wide variety of performing, visual, and literary arts, and seeks to present the best Utah artists and their contemporaries worldwide. The Festival presents several core events annually: an Artists Marketplace, a Culinary Arts Program, and a Performing Arts Program. The Festival augments these core events each year with new and creative programs, artists, performances, and site elements, thereby ensuring each event is an innovative and unique celebration of the arts. To preserve its reputation for artistic excellence, all artistic work presented by the Utah Arts Festival is either juried or curated by professional artists and arts administrators.

The Utah Arts Festival's programming emphasizes contemporary art.

The Utah Arts Festival's emphasis on contemporary art implies a willingness to accept artistic risk by presenting artists, forms and subject matter that are innovative or non-traditional, provided that work is seen to adhere to critical standards of aesthetic quality and overall artistic integrity. In all artistic media and genre, the Festival encourages among its patrons an appreciation of and interest in fine art. The Utah Arts Festival fosters the creation of new artwork through competitions and commissions to artists and desires, whenever possible, to be a premier venue for introducing artists to Utah audiences. The Festival also values the interaction of patrons with artists, and seeks to provide opportunities for dialogue and education, both within the artistic community and between artists and the general public.

Best of the Northwest

Show dates for 2003:
Seattle–May 9, 10, 11; August 16 & 17; November 21, 22, 23;
Portland–November 14, 15, 16
info@bestnwcrafts.com
(360) 221-6191

Best of the Northwest's selected artists bring an exciting mix of Northwest art and unique and functional crafts in metal, glass and wood sculpture, jewelry, wearable art, pottery, photography, mixed media, fiber arts, and basketry to satisfy a wide variety of tastes and budgets.

The mission of Northwest Crafts Alliance is to promote Northwest artists and their work through 4 shows a year. Our Seattle shows in the spring and fall are held in an historic airplane hanger at Sand Point Magnuson Park, 7400 Sand Point Way NE. We have free show parking at Sand Point. Our summer Seattle show is free and outdoors at Sand Point Magnuson Park. The Oregon Convention Center, 777 NE Martin Luther King Jr. Blvd. is the venue for our fall Portland Show.

For more information and 2004 dates, contact our office at PO Box 1057 Clinton, WA 98236, Phone: (360) 221-6191.

UW Summer Arts Festival

July 16–19, 2003
University of Washington Campus
Seattle, Washington
www.summerartsfest.org
for information, (206) 685-6696
for tickets, (206) 543-4880
Ticket prices range from $8 to $35; Some events are free

This summer the University of Washington hosts its fourth annual Summer Arts Festival—a unique opportunity to enjoy performances, exhibitions, screenings, workshops, readings and symposia contemplating the theme, *Spheres*. From Leonardo Da Vinci's *Vitruvian Man* to Buckminster Fuller's geodesic dome, humans have been tantalized by the seductiveness of the circular form. Let the 2003 UW Summer Arts Festival ignite your imagination as it explores *Spheres* in a celebration of art, history and science. Dedicated to the role of education and the arts, the Festival also offers a variety of workshops in the arts for young people.

Special guests include the Seattle Repertory Jazz Orchestra, Psychograss, the Chamber Dance Company, Linda Bierds, David Wagoner, Ron Moore, Perry Lorenzo and the Northwest Premiere of Kronos Quartet's *Sun Rings*.

Directions: The Seattle campus of the University of Washington is located at the intersection of NE 45th Street and 15th Avenue NE, just a few miles north of downtown Seattle.

Washington State International Kite Festival

August 18–25, 2003
Long Beach, Washington
www.kitefestival.com
(800) 451-2542

The Washington State International Kite Festival fills the sky above Long Beach with kites of all sizes, shapes and colors. The Festival takes place annually during the third full week of August in Long Beach, WA. This year the festival begins on Monday, August 18, and goes through Sunday, August 25.

Long Beach is located near the mouth of the Columbia River on the Pacific Ocean where it is subject to steady northwest winds-and August is perfect for kites! Every year, thousand of people from all over the world gather here to participate and watch the kites. Kites from the smallest to the largest in the world have been flown here. Every day there are scheduled events that are open to the public. There are 50 or more vendors that the festival with everything from food to arts and crafts. Come and join us for some family fun! More details are available on our Web site!

Warrens Cranberry Festival

September 26–28, 2003
Warrens, Wisconsin
www.cranfest.com
(608) 378-4200

The 31st annual Warrens Cranberry Festival will be held September 26–28, 2003. The festival kicks off with the art & craft show, flea & antique market, and farmers market at 7:00 A.M. all three days.

There is a variety of contests for young and old alike. Contest rules are available from the Cranberry Festival office for needlework, scarecrow, flower, vegetable & sunflower, cap & hat, photography, and the Wisconsin Cranberry Recipe Contest. All contests take place at the Elementary School and are on display through Sunday of the festival. Kitchen Craft-West Bend food demos will be held Friday through Sunday.

- The Family Variety Time is Friday and Saturday afternoon, and Saturday evening in the Old Towne Hall, sit down and be entertained. Listen to old time gospel and a variety of music. Musicians are throughout the grounds during the weekend with flute music of the Andes, piano and dulcimer.
- Saturday only, hop aboard a bus for a Cranberry Marsh/Ocean Spray Receiving Station tour beginning at 8:30 A.M. Purchase your ticket at the Municipal Building on George Street. This is a two-hour guided tour.
- The gigantic parade is held on Sunday starting at 1:00 P.M., come early and bring your lawn chair.

Festivals Directory

West Region

Alaska

Arizona

California

Colorado

Hawaii

Idaho

Montana

Nevada

New Mexico

Oregon

Utah

Washington

Midwest Region

Illinois

Indiana

Iowa

Kansas

Michigan

Minnesota

Missouri

Nebraska

North Dakota

Ohio

South Dakota

Wisconsin

South Region

Alabama

Arkansas

Delaware

Florida

Georgia

Kentucky

Louisiana

Maryland

Mississippi

North Carolina

Oklahoma

South Carolina

Tennessee

Texas

Virginia

W. Virginia

Washington DC

East Region

Connecticut

Maine

Massachusetts

New Hampshire

New Jersey

New York

Pennsylvania

Rhode Island

Vermont

Alaska

Anchorage Fur Rendezvous

Anchorage, Alaska
February 14–23, 2003
www.furrondy.net
907-274-1177

Winter fun & frolicking, sled dog race, native arts & crafts, Masque Ball.

Bear Paw Festival

Eagle River, Alaska
July 9–13, 2003
www.cer.org
907-694-4702

Bear Paw Rocks-n-Rolls with contests, chili cook-off, quilt show & auction.

Fairbanks Summer Arts Festival

Fairbanks, Alaska
February 13–27, 2003
www.fsaf.org
907-474-8869

A study-performance Festival with guest artists who teach & perform.

Iditarod Trail Sled Dog Race

Nome, Alaska
March 1–18, 2003
www.iditarod.com
907-376-5155

The world's longest sled dog race mingled with food, crafts & fun events.

Arizona

2003 Thunderbird Balloon Classic

Scottsdale, Arizona
November 14–16, 2003
www.t-birdballoonclassic.com
602-978-7797

Colorful morning launches & evening glows, skydiving, family activities.

Arizona Renaissance Festival and Artisan Marketplace

Apache Junction, Arizona
February 1 – March 23, 2003
www.royalfaires.com
520-463-2700

Revel in the atmosphere of a 16th Century European Country Faire.

Carefree Fine Art and Wine Festival

Carefree, Arizona
February 28 – March 2, 2003
www.ThunderbirdArtists.com
480-837-5637

A spectacular gathering of arts, wines, gourmet food, & chocolates.

Cave Creek Spring Arts and Crafts Festival

Cave Creek, Arizona
February 15–17, 2003
www.ckevents.com
623-842-8434

A juried arts & crafts event with a Wild West flair.

Celebration of Fine Art

Scottsdale, Arizona
January 11 – March 23, 2003
www.celebrateart.com
480-443-7695

Working artists' studios, hand-made furniture & life-sized sculpture.

Chandler Ostrich Festival

Chandler, Arizona
March 7–9, 2003
www.ostrichfestival.com
623-842-8434

World famous ostrich races, arts & crafts, unique ostrich products.

Cinco de Mayo Festival

Phoenix, Arizona
May 2–4, 2003
www.arvizu.com
602-279-4669

Hispanic cultural event, featuring national & regional entertainment.

Cochise Cowboy Poetry and Music Gathering

Featured on page 4

Sierra Vista, Arizona
early February
www.cowboypoets.com
800-288-3861

Enjoy this tribute to cowboy tradition; storytellers, poets, singers & musicians

Festival of the West

Scottsdale, Arizona
March 13–16, 2003
www.festivalofthewest.com
602-996-4387

American West celebration, western entertainment, cook off, cowboy poetry.

Fourth Avenue Street Fair

Tucson, Arizona
March 21–32, 2003
www.fourthavenue.org
520-624-5004

Arts & crafts, music stages, street performers on the tree-lined streets.

Glendale Chocolate Affaire

Glendale, Arizona
February 7–9, 2003
www.glendaleaz.com
623-930-2299

Upscale festival with horse-drawn carriage rides, tours of Cerreta Candy Co.

Gold Rush Days

Wickenburg, Arizona
February 14–16, 2003
www.wickenburgchamber.com
928-684-5479

Celebration of ranching & mining heritage, gold-panning, rodeo, parade.

La Fiesta de los Vaqueros

Tucson, Arizona
February 16–23, 2003
www.tucsonrodeo.com
520-741-2233

Outdoor mid-winter rodeo & the largest non-motorized parade in the world.

MAMA Fall Festival of the Arts

Tempe, Arizona
December 5–7, 2003
phoenix.about.com
480-967-4877

Annual arts & crafts festival held downtown, features artists & entertainment.

Scottsdale Fine Art and Chocolate Festival

Scottsdale, Arizona
February 7–9, 2003
thunderbirdartists.com
480-837-5637

A can't miss event for any art or chocolate lover at the Scottsdale Pavilions.

Way Out West Oktoberfest

Tempe, Arizona
October 3–5, 2003
www.tempe.gov/sister
480-491-FEST (3378)

Features Bavarian polka music, country western music, family entertainment.

Worlds Oldest Continuous PRCA Rodeo

Payson, Arizona
August 15–17, 2003
www.rimcountrychamber.com
800- 672-9766

The World's Oldest Continuous Rodeo, running continuously since 1884.

California

Africamix Festival

Sacramento, CA
June 28–29, 2003
www.africamix.org
800-456-1116

Diverse artists, musicians, guest speakers from children's rights organizations.

Arcata Bay Oyster Festival

Arcata, California
June 14, 2003
arcata.com/chamber
707-822-4500

Local chefs & caterers celebrate oysters, Oyster calling contest, Farmer's Market.

Big Hat Days

Clovis, California
April 5–6, 2003
www.clovischamber.com
559 299-7363

A fun festival that includes craft booths, car show, carnival, home & garden show.

Blockbuster Hollywood Spectacular

Hollywood, California
November 30, 2003
hollywoodchristmas.com
323-469-2337

Parade featuring floats, marching bands, celebrities, costumed characters.

Bodega Bay Seafood, Art and Wine Festival

Bodega Bay, California
August 23–24, 2003
www.sonomawetlands.org
707-824-8404

Enjoy seafood & other edibles, wines & microbrews, art & entertainment.

Bok Kai Festival

Marysville, California
March 8–9, 2003
janec@jps.net
530-743-4151

Features a parade & activities honoring Bok Kai, the Chinese Water God.

Calabasas Pumpkin Festival

Agoura, California
October 18–19, 2003
www.pumpkin-festival.com
818-222-5680

Tons of pumpkins, pie eating & seed spitting contests, pumpkin bowling.

California Avocado Festival

Carpinteria, California
October 3–5, 2003
www.avofest.com
805-684-0038

Celebrates the versatility of the avocado with hundreds of Avo-tivities.

California Country Music Festival

Mariposa, California
May 24–26, 2003
www.calcountryfest.com
661-299-4871

Features some of country music's stars, overnight camping, unique attractions.

California Dried Plum Festival

Yuba City, California
September 6–7, 2003
www.prunefestival.org
530-671-3100

Arts & crafts, artisans village, farmers market, parade, tempting prune dishes.

California Dry Bean Festival

Tracy, California
August 2–3, 2003
tracychamber.org
209-835-2131

Family event with arts & crafts, kid's area, great food, & commercial exhibits.

California International Airshow

Salinas, California
October 3–5, 2003
www.salinasairshow.com
888-845-7469

Military demonstrations, fireworks, entertainment from the ground up.

California Kidsfaire

Pleasanton, California
September 14, 2003
www.thekidsfaire.com
866-444-3976

Interactive fun booths, games, rides, magicians, clowns, non-stop family fun.

California Mid Winter Fair and Fiesta

Imperial, California
February 28 – March 9, 2003
www.ivexpo.com
760-355-1181

Livestock auction, community exhibits, speedway races, petting zoo, fun for all.

California Peach Festival

Marysville, California
July 19, 2003
www.capeachfestival.com
530-671-9600

A peaches & pancake breakfast, children's activities, plus a 5K Run/Walk.

California Shakespeare Festival

Orinda, California
May 28 – October 5, 2003
www.calshakes.org
510-548-9666

Great works come alive. Shakespeare &classic plays, discussion forums.

Carnaval San Francisco Parade and Festival

San Francisco, California
May 24–25, 2003
www.carnavalsf.com
415-920-0125

Carnaval King & Queen reign & spectacular groups dazzle in Mardi Gras style.

Chalk La Strada Streetpainting Festival

San Diego, California
October 18–19, 2003
www.chalklastrada.com
877-362-4255

Streetpainters chalk up the streets, free entertainment, Italian festa, & vendors.

Cherry Blossom Festival

San Francisco, California
April 19–27, 2003
415-563-2313

Festival displays Japanese food, music, martial arts, performers, & a parade.

Chinese New Year Festival and Parade

San Francisco, California
January 25 – February 16, 2003
www.chineseparade.com
415-391-9680

Flower Market Fair, Miss Chinatown pageant, street fair & dragon parade.

Cowboy Poetry and Music Festival

Santa Clarita, California
March 26–30, 2003
www.santa-clarita.com/cp
800-305-0755

The late Gene Autry's Melody Ranch hosts musicians, poets, & storytellers.

Crossroads Street Faire

Manteca, California
April 5–6, 2003
www.manteca.org/cvb
209 823-7229

Tree-lined streets offer arts & crafts, antiques, commercial products, food.

Día de Los Muertos Fruitvale Festival

Oakland, California
October 26, 2003
www.unitycouncil.org
510-535-6900

A culturally diverse event featuring Latino music, dance, art & activities.

Doo Dah Parade

Pasadena, California
November 23, 2003
www.pasadenadoodahparade.com
626-440-7379

Spoof on the Pasadena Rose Parade with boisterous, wacky participants.

Encinitas Oktoberfest and Craft Faire

Encinitas, California
September 28, 2003
www.encinitaschamber.com
760-632-1199

Street fair & German celebration, oompah bands, storytelling, dancing.

Fallbrook Avocado Festival

Fallbrook, California
April 13, 2003
www.fallbrookca.org
760-728-5845

Guacamole recipe contest, games, vendors, packing plant tours, family fun.

Festival of Arts

Laguna Beach, California
July 6 – August 29, 2003
www.foapom.com
949-494-1145

Area artists represent a complete spectrum of media, original art.

Festival of Philippine Arts and Culture

San Pedro, California
September 6–7, 2003
www.filamarts.org
213-389-3050

Filipino American creative spirit in dance, music, theater, visual arts.

Festival of the Arts and Food Faire

La Jolla, California
June 14–15, 2003
www.lajollaartfestival.org
619-645-8484

A gathering of specially selected artists, superb food & live entertainment.

Festival of Whales

Dana Point, California
March 8–16, 2003
www.festivalofwhales.org
888-440-4309

Whale watching, YMCA Whale Run, Ocean Awareness, water sports exhibits.

Fremont Festival of the Arts

Fremont, California
July 26–27, 2003
www.fremontfestival.net
510-795-4781

Artisans, music, food & beverage booths with entertainers & fun for all.

Garden Grove Strawberry Festival

Garden Grove, California
May 23–26, 2003
www.strawberryfestival.org
714-638-0981

This community fair features carnival rides, game booths, shows, parade.

Gilroy Garlic Festival

Featured on page 6

Gilroy, California
July 25–27, 2003
www.gilroygarlicfestival.com
408-842-1625

Garlic recipe contest & cook off, ethnic foods, entertainment.

Golden Dragon Parade and Chinatown Street Fair

Los Angeles, California
February 15, 2003
www.lachinesechamber.org
213-617-0396

A traditional, colorful parade celebrates the Chinese New Year.

Half Moon Bay Art and Pumpkin Festival

Half Moon Bay, California
October 18–19, 2003
www.miramarevents.com
650-726-9652
Pumpkin patches, harvest-inspired arts & crafts, Great Pumpkin Parade.

Hayward - Russell City Blues Festival

Featured on page 7
July 12–13, 2003
www.geocities.com/hipwayblues
510-836-2227 or 707-647-3962
Blues history of Russell City in festival, lecture and archival musical showings.

Horned Toad Derby

Coalinga, California
May 23–26, 2003
www.coalingachamber.com
800-854-3885
Horned toad races, carnival, parade, fireman's water fights, entertainment.

Indio International Tamale Festival

Indio, California
December 6–7, 2003
www.tamalefestival.org
760-342-6532
Every imaginable kind of tamale–a traditional holiday treat–Christmas crafts.

International Family Festival

Modesto, California
October 4–5, 2003
www.geocities.com/internationalfestivalmodesto
209-521-3852
Celebrates the region's cultural diversity through food, dance, music, & art.

Isleton Crawdad Festival

Isleton, California
June 13–15, 2003
isletoncoc.org
916-777-5880
Some 22,000 lbs. of crawdads, contests, crawdad races, Cajun music.

Johnny Appleseed Days

Paradise, California
October 4–5, 2003
www.paradisechamber.com
530-877-9356
Celebrates the fruit harvest with everything apple, crafts, pancake breakfast.

Kites Over Pismo

Pismo Beach, California
October 18–19, 2003
www.pismokites.com
805-474-8442
Stunt kite demos, spectator flying zone, Teddy Bear parachuting & candy drops.

La Habra Corn Festival

La Habra, California
August 1–3, 2003
www.lahabrahostlions.homestead.com
562-243-2417

Festival features great food, games, craft displays, & carnival rides.

La Mesa Oktoberfest

La Mesa, California
October 3–5, 2003
www.eastcountychamber.org
619-440-6161

Features a beer garden with Bavarian entertainment & bratwurst!

La Quinta Arts Festival

La Quinta, California
March 20–23, 2003
www.lqaf.com
760-564-1244

Pre-eminent artists, fine wines, entertainment, hands-on activities.

Lodi Grape Festival and Harvest Fair

Lodi, California
September 18–21, 2003
www.grapefestival.com
209-369-2771

Competitive exhibits of art, floriculture, & agriculture, grape stomps & parade.

Long Beach Blues Festival

Long Beach, California
August 30 – September 1, 2003
www.kkjz.org/events
562-985-5566

The finest national blues performers in jumpin' stage concerts & plenty of sun.

Long Beach Chili Cook-off (Formerly Beach Fest)

Long Beach, California
June 7–8, 2003
www.LongBeachChiliCookoff.com
877-669-2552

"World famous" chili cook-off, Salsa Challenge, Buffalo Wing competition.

Los Altos Arts and Wine Festival

Los Altos, California
July 12–13, 2003
losaltos-downtown.org
650-917-9799

Picturesque village fills with fine art, premium wines & microbrews, Kidzone.

Los Angeles Times Festival of Books

Los Angeles, California
April 26–27, 2003
www.latimes.com/festivalofbooks
800-528-4637 ext. 7BOOK

Renowned authors, book signings, LA Times Book Prizes, diverse exhibits.

Mammoth Lakes Jazz Jubilee

Mammoth Lakes, California
July 10–13, 2003
www.mammothjazz.org
760-964-2478

Great traditional jazz & spectacular High Sierra views equals one giant jazz buzz.

MCAS Miramar Airshow

San Diego, California
October 17–19, 2003
www.miramarairshow.com
858-577-6365

World-class, award-winning military & civilian show, displays, fireworks.

Mendocino Music Festival

Mendocino, California
July 15–26, 2003
www.mendocinomusic.com
707-937-2044

Lulling surf mixes with music; opera, rehearsals & pre-concert lectures.

Monterey Bay Blues Festival

Monterey, California
June 27–29, 2003
www.montereyblues.com
831-394-2652

Electrifying blues performers, such as Kenny Neal & Etta James.

Monterey Bay Strawberry Festival in Watsonville

Watsonville, California
August 2–3, 2003
ejaworowski@tpnco.com
831.728.6183

Delectable strawberry delights, gooey contests for berry lovers, arts & crafts.

Monterey Jazz Festival Presented by WorldCom

Monterey, California
September 19–21, 2003
www.montereyjazzfestival.org
831-373-3366

World's finest jazz musicians, exhibits, workshops, jazz conversation areas.

Mountain Mandarin Festival

Auburn, California
November 22–23, 2003
www.mandarinfestival.com
916-663-1918

Celebrate agriculture & the popular & locally grown mandarin orange.

NoHo Theatre and Arts Festival

North Hollywood, California
May 17–18, 2003
www.nohoartsdistrict.com
818 508 5155

Live theater, music, dance, Kids Kourt, arts & crafts, international cuisine.

Nortel Networks Palm Springs International Film Festival

Palm Springs, California
January 6–20, 2003
www.psfilmfest.org
800-898-7256

The best of international cinema, guest appearances, seminars, panels.

Oakley Almond Festival

Oakley, California
September 13–14, 2003
www.oakleychamber.com/festival
925-625-1035

Be almond amazed! Almond Parade, recipe contests, Almondland for kids.

Ojai Music Festival

Ojai, California
May 28 – June 1, 2003
www.ojaifestival.org
805-646-2094

A highly sophisticated, classical program performed in a small & rustic setting.

Old Pasadena Summer Festival

Pasadena, California
May 24–26, 2003
delmanoprod.com/opsmfst
626-797-6803

Come for fun & music, stay for the food & flavors.

Old Spanish Days Fiesta

Santa Barbara, California
July 30 – August 3, 2003
www.oldspanishdays-fiesta.org
805-962-8101

Grande parade, horse-drawn carriages, Spanish markets, dancing, shows.

Pan African Film and Arts Festival

Los Angeles, California
February 5–17, 2003
www.paff.org
323-295-1706

Premier Black film festival in the U.S., children's films, StudentFest, art show.

Pittsburg Seafood Festival

Pittsburg, California
September 6–7, 2003
www.pittsburg.org
925-432-7301

Seafood specialties from local restaurants, beer garden, wine pavilion..

Port of Los Angeles Lobster Festival

San Pedro, California
October 3–5, 2003
www.lobsterfest.com
310-366-6472

A celebration of the cultural heritage of the city's maritime beginnings.

Redondo Beach Lobster Festival

Redondo Beach, California
September 26–28, 2003
www.redondochamber.org
888-465-5488

Come for the lobsters (& other fine foods), stay for the fun on the beach.

Redwood Coast Dixieland Jazz Festival

Eureka, California
March 28–30, 2003
www.redwoodjazz.org
707-445-3378

Non-stop music features some of the world's best jazz bands.

Renaissance Pleasure Faire

Casa de Fruta
September 13 – October 19, 2003
www.renfair.com
800-523-2473

lively re-creation of 16th century English marketplace & Harvest Festival.

Riverside County Fair & National Date Festival

Indio, California
February 14–23, 2003
www.datefest.org
800-811-3247

Headliner entertainment, pageant, camel & ostrich races, monster trucks.

Route 66 Rendezvous

San Bernardino, California
September 18–21, 2003
www.route-66.org
800-867-8366

Cruise on down! A park 'n' cruise route, cruisin' contests & pre-1973 cruisin' cars.

Russian River Blues Festival

Guerneville, California
June 28–29, 2003
www.russianriverbluesfest.com
510-655-9471

A collection of top blues greats take center stage at Johnson's Beach.

Sabor de Mexico Lindo

Huntington Park, California
October 3–5, 2003
hpchamber1.com
323-585-1155

Celebrate Mexican Heritage Month with food, contests, petting zoo, arts & crafts.

Sacramento Jazz Jubilee

Sacramento, California
May 23–26, 2003
www.sacjazz.com
916-372-5277

Features traditional jazz, other music genres, & our popular Children's Stage.

San Anselmo Art Festival

San Anselmo, California
June 21–22, 2003
www.hartmannstudios.com
510-970-3217

Fine arts & crafts, jazz, family entertainment, amidst abundant antique dealers.

San Carlos Art And Wine Faire

San Carlos, California
October 10, 2003
www.sancarloschamber.org
650-593-1068

Juried art show, food, beer & wine tasting & live entertainment.

San Clemente Ocean Festival

San Clemente, California
July 19–20, 2003
www.oceanfestival.org
949-440-6141

Celebrate sun, fun & surf, athletic events & clinics, surf music, art exhibition.

San Diego Street Scene

San Diego, California
September 5–7, 2003
www.street-scene.com
619-557-8490

Performances of the best in rock, reggae, alternative, jazz, funk, zydeco, Cajun.

San Francisco Blues Festival

San Francisco, California
September 27–28, 2003
www.sfblues.com
415-979-5588

An eclectic mix of urban, rural, acoustic & electric blues, with spectacular views.

San Francisco Examiner Bay to Breakers

San Francisco, California
May 18, 2003
www.baytobreakers.com
415-808-5000 x2222

The largest foot race in the world, a post-race festival, concert, food & beverages.

San Jose Holiday Parade

Featured on page 8

San Jose, California
December 7, 2003
www.sanjoseholidayparade.com
408-277-3303

Parade & festivities include animated displays, special activities & exhibits.

San Jose Jazz Festival

San Jose, California
August 6–10, 2003
www.sanjosejazz.org
408-288-7557

Richly diverse jazz styles, local, regional, national & international musicians.

San Leandro Sausage and Suds Music Festival

San Leandro, California
October 5, 2003
www.sanleandrochamber.com
510-357-3322

Some of the Bay Area's most talented musicians, local sausage & beer vendors.

Santa Barbara French Festival

Santa Barbara, California
July 12–13, 2003
www.frenchfestival.com
805-564-7274

Oo la la! A huge French celebration! The Eiffel Tower, entertainment, vendors.

Santa Barbara International Film Festival

Santa Barbara, California
February 28 – March 9, 2003
www.sbfilmfestival.org
805-963-0023

Seminars, tributes, galas, diverse programming & noteworthy discoveries.

Santa Barbara Whale Festival

Santa Barbara, California
March 29–30, 2003
www.sbwhalefestival.com
805-897-3187

A fun & educational festival coinciding with northern migration of gray whales.

Santa Clara Art and Wine Festival

Santa Clara, California
September 13–14, 2003
ci.santa-clara.ca.us
408-984-3257

Artists, tantalizing foods, entertainment & Kids' Kingdom in Central Park.

Santa Maria Elk's Rodeo & Parade

Featured on page 5

Santa Maria, California
June 5–8, 2003
www.elks1538.com
805-922-6006

Experience roundup thrills, calf-roping, barrel-racing, mutton-bustin', cowboys.

Sausalito Art Festival

Sausalito, California
August 29 – September 1, 2003
www.sausalitoartfest.org
415-331-3757

Juried art show, Sculpture Garden, concert, children's theater, gourmet foods.

Sawdust Art Festival

Laguna Beach, California
June 28 – August 31, 2003
sawdustartfestival.org
949 494-3030

A unique fine art & creative craft show in a sawdust-covered eucalyptus grove.

Silverado Days

Buena Park, California
October 16–19, 2003
www.silveradodays.com
714-562-3560

Silverado Charity Ball, Chili Cook-Off, Silverado Days Parade, ongoing events.

Sonoma County Harvest Festival

Santa Rosa, California
October 3–5, 2003
www.harvestfair.org
707-545-4203

Celebrate grape harvest, wine tasting, grape stomp, jazz music, arts & crafts.

Stagecoach Days

Banning, California
October 2–5, 2003
stagecoachdays.com
909-849-9626

Civil War re-enactments with drill demos, officer's families, field hospitals.

Stater Bros. Riverside Orange Blossom Festival

Riverside, California
April 12–13, 2003
www.orangeblossomfestival.org
909-715-3400

Parade, exploration activities for kids, music, top chefs creating orange dishes.

Steinbeck Festival

Salinas, California
August 7–10, 2003
www.steinbeck.org
831-775-4720

Lectures, presentations, films, tours & trips to Steinbeck locales, dinner events.

Stern Grove Festival

San Francisco, California
June 1 – August 1, 2003
www.sterngrove.org
415-252-6252

Performing arts featuring contemporary & classical artists, natural amphitheater.

Stockton Asparagus Festival

Stockton, California
April 25–27, 2003
www.asparagusfest.com
209-943-1987

Asparagus Celebrity Kitchen & Asparagus Alley, a variety of music & treats.

Sunnyvale Art and Wine Festival

Sunnyvale, California
June 7–8, 2003
www.svcoc.org
408-736-4971

Artists & craftspeople, local wineries & microbreweries, food, entertainment.

Tapestry Arts Festival

San Jose, California
August 30 – September 1, 2003
tapestryintalent.org
408-494-3590

Artists, delicious foods, hands-on art activities, home & garden show.

Taste of Morgan Hill, 14th Annual

Morgan Hill, California
September 27–28, 2003
www.morganhill.org/tasteofmh
408-779-9444

Local restaurants, microbrew & wine garden, car show, arts & crafts.

Taste of Newport

Newport Beach, California
September 12–14, 2003
tasteofnewport.com
949-729-4400

The area's social event of the year! Restaurants, wines & brews, entertainment.

Tehachapi Mountain Festival

Tehachapi, California
August 16–17, 2003
www.tehachapi.com
661-822-4180

Parade, carnival, rodeo queen events, PRCA rodeo, fine arts, evening dance.

Temecula Valley Balloon and Wine Festival

Temecula, California
June 6–8, 2003
www.tvbwf.com
909-676-6713

Treat yourself to balloons soaring high & internationally known musicians.

Tournament of Roses Parade

Pasadena, California
January 1, 2003
www.tournamentofroses.com
626-449-7673

Floral floats, marching bands, equestrians & a Thunderbirds fly-over.

Travis Air Force Base Air Expo

Travis AFB, California
June 14–15, 2003
www.travisairexpo.com
707-424-0134

See the pride & power of America's military aircraft in action.

Upland Lemon Festival

Upland, California
April 2, 3003
culturalcenter.org/lemon
909-949-4499

Lemons abound, vendors compete, arts & crafts, children's fair, fireworks.

Uptown Arts and Crafts Street Festival

Whittier, California
July 12–13, 2002
www.whittieruptown.org
562-696-2662

Craftspeople, food booths, live entertainment & a $5000 cash raffle.

Van Nuys Airport Aviation Expo

Van Nuys, California
June 21–22, 2003
www.lawa.org/vny/
818-773-3293

Displays of military & vintage aircraft, exciting flyovers, pilots sign autographs.

Watsonville Fly-In and Air Show

Watsonville, California
May 23–25, 2003
www.watsonvilleflyin.org
831 763-5600

Vintage & homebuilt aircraft, dazzling performers & fabulous flying machines.

West Hollywood Halloween Carnaval

West Hollywood, California
October 31, 2003
www.visitwesthollywood.com
310-289-2525

Outdoor Halloween celebration features top entertainment, creative costumes.

Whiskey Flat Days

Kernville, California
February 14–17, 2003
www.kernvalley.com/news/whiskey.htm
760-376-2629

Back to the 1860s: frog races, wood carving, whiskerino contest, dances, rodeo.

World Pillow Fighting Championships

Kenwood, California
July 4, 2003
www.kenwoodpillowfights.com
707-833-2440

Unabashed joy & silliness prevail with pillow fights, live bands, great food.

Colorado

Aspen Music Festival

Aspen, Colorado
June 19 – August 17, 2003
www.aspenmusicfestival.com
970-925-3254

Concerts on the mountain & in town concert hall, students & mentors together.

AT&T LoDo Music Festival

Denver, Colorado
July 18–19, 2003
www.lodomusicfestival.com
303-295-1195

Spectacular music, street performers, drum circle, unique food & art vendors

Bravo! Vail Valley Music Festival

Vail, Colorado
June 27 – August 5, 2003
www.vailmusicfestival.org
877-827-5700

Chamber music, orchestra & jazz performances at breathtaking venues.

Carnival! and The Mumbo Jumbo Gumbo Cook-off

Manitou Springs, Colorado
March 1, 2003
manitou@pikes-peak.com
800-642-2567

Mardi Gras-style celebration features a parade, Cajun music, dance, food

Cherry Creek Arts Festival

Denver, Colorado
July 4–6, 2003
www.cherryarts.org
303-355-2787

Every means of artistic expression, top performance artists & musicians.

Chili and Frijole Festival

Pueblo, Colorado
September 19–21, 2003
www.pueblochamber.org
800-233-3446

Artists, entertainers, contests, arts & crafts, farmers' market, cooking demos.

Colorado Performing Arts Festival

Denver, Colorado
September 28–29, 2003
www.denvergov.org
303-640-6943

Colorado-based performing artists & groups in dance, music, theatre.

Colorado Renaissance Festival

Larkspur, Colorado
June 14 – August 3, 2003
www.coloradorenaissance.com
303-688-6010

Master revelers reign, magical entertainments, games of skill, period arts.

Colorado Shakespeare Festival

Boulder, Colorado
June 26 – August 24, 2003
www.coloradoshakes.org
303-492-1527

The second oldest Shakespeare festival in the U.S.

Colorado Springs Balloon Classic

Colorado Springs, Colorado
August 30 – September 1, 2003
www.balloonclassic.com
719-471-4833

Colorful hot air balloons, concessions, demonstrations, & great entertainment.

Downtown Denver International Buskerfest

Denver, Colorado
June 20–22, 2003
www.buskerfest.com
303-478-7878

Premier street performers featuring jugglers, acrobats, sword swallowing.

Festival of Mountain and Plain–A Taste of Colorado

Denver, Colorado
August 29 – September 1, 2003
www.downtowndenver.com
303-478-7878

Food & entertainment extravaganza features gourmet cooking demos, music.

Great American Beer Festival

Denver, Colorado
September 25–27, 2003
www.beertown.org
303-447-0816

Celebrates American brewing with industry experts' awards, seminars, tastings.

Greeley Independence Stampede

Greeley, Colorado
June 26 – July 6, 2003
www.greeleystampede.org
970-356-7787

PRCA rodeo, nightly music, parade, fireworks, flapjack & watermelon feeds.

Loveland Corn Roast Festival

Loveland, Colorado
August 22–23, 2003
www.loveland.org
970-667-6311

Corn shucking contests, concert, parade, duck dace, pancake breakfast, bull riding.

Oktoberfest on Larimer Square

Denver, Colorado
September 18–21, 2003
www.larimerarts.org
303-534-2367

Authentic German food, entertainment, Bier Garten, Kinderplatz.

Parker Country Festival

Parker, Colorado
June 13–15, 2003
www.parkerchamber.com
303-841-4268

A variety of bands plus great food, games & fun for the kids.

Strawberry Days Festival

Glenwood Springs, Colorado
June 20–22, 2003
www.strawberrydaysfestival.com
970-945-6589

Arts, food, KidsFest activities & one day of free strawberries & ice cream!

Telluride Bluegrass Festival

Telluride, Colorado
June 19–22, 2003
www.bluegrass.com
303-823-0848

An exquisitely eclectic weekend of acoustic music from around the planet.

Telluride Blues and Brews Festival

Telluride, Colorado
September 12–14, 2003
tellurideblues.com
866-515-6166

National blues acts combined with a Grand Beer Tasting on Saturday.

Hawaii

Aloha Festivals Hawaii

Honolulu, Hawaii
September 12 – October 29, 2003
www.alohafestivals.com
808-589-1771

Cultural cornucopia of the islands with cultural & historical programs.

Hawaii's Big Island Festival

Kailua-Kona, Hawaii
November 5-9, 2003
bigislandfestival.com
266-424-3378

A celebration of diversity, cuisine, culture, healing and music.

Taste of Honolulu

Honolulu, Hawaii
June 20–22, 2003
www.eastersealshawaii.org/taste
808-536-1015

Premier restaurants' signature dishes, wines, microbrews, entertainment.

The Great Maui Whale Festival

Wailuku, Hawaii
December 1, 2002 – May 15, 2003
www.pacificwhale.org
808-249-8811

This fun festival honors the presence of humpback whales in Maui's waters.

Idaho

Boise River Festival

Featured on page 12

Boise, Idaho
June 27–29, 2003
www.boiseriverfestival.org
208-338-8887

Musical entertainment, craft show, sporting events, fireworks grand finale.

Idaho International Folk Dance Festival

Rexburg, Idaho
July 26 – August 2, 2003
www.rexcc.com/festival
208-356-5700

Dancers & musicians from around the world create a folk village atmosphere.

Lionel Hampton Jazz Festival

Moscow, Idaho
February 19–22, 2003
www.jazz.uidaho.edu
208-885-6765

Student competitions, artist workshops, master classes, concerts.

National Oldtime Fiddlers' Contest and Festival

Weiser, Idaho
June 16–21, 2003
www.fiddlecontest.com
800-437-1280

The town plays host to title competitions, nonstop jam sessions, arts, crafts.

Montana

Mount Helena Music Festival

Helena, Montana
June 20–22, 2003
www.downtownhelena.com
406-447-1535

A variety of music, arts, & fun for the enjoyment & participation of all ages.

Race to the Sky

Helena, Montana
February 8–13, 2003
www.race2sky.com
406-442-4008

A challenging 350-mile race along the Continental Divide.

Testicle Festival

Clinton, Montana
September 17–21, 2003
www.testyfesty.com
406-825-4868

Secret recipe bull testicles (Rocky Mountain Oysters), eclectic people; adults only.

Nevada

Best in the West Nugget Rib Cook-off

Sparks, Nevada
August 28 – September 1, 2003
www.janugget.com/events
775-353-2291

Rib cookers from across the country compete for the title & sell their ribs.

Burning Man Festival

Black Rock City, Nevada
August 25 – September 1, 2003
www.burningman.com
415-985-7471

A wild & dangerous self-reliance & survival weekend. Be prepared.

Hot August Nights

Reno, Nevada
August 3–10, 2003
www.hotaugustnights.net
775-356-1956

A celebration of America's love affair with cars & rock & roll.

National Championship Air Races and Airshow

Reno, Nevada
September 11–14, 2003
www.airrace.org
775-972-6663

This show is so big, it needs the heavens as its stage.

Reno Jazz Festival

Featured on page 22

Reno, Nevada
May 1–3, 2003
www.unr.edu
775-784-4046

Instrumental & vocal competitions, clinics & evening concerts.

San Gennaro Feast

Las Vegas, Nevada
September 10–14, 2003
sangennarofeast.net
702 286-4944

A popular feast for the palate & loads of fun at the carnival & midway.

Tahoe International Spring SnowFest

North Lake Tahoe, Nevada
February 28 – March 9, 2003
joylemdoyl@aol.com
775-832-7625

Downhill ski races, cross country race, polar bear swim, snow sculpture.

Tri-County Fair & Stampede

Featured on page 23

Winnemucca, Nevada
August 29–31, 2003
www.winnemucca.nv.us
775-623-5071

Parade, carnival, gold panning, rodeo, parade, demolition derby, ATV pulls.

New Mexico

Gathering of Nations Powwow

Albuquerque, New Mexico
April 24–26, 2003
www.gatheringofnations.com
505-836-2810

Singers & dancers from more than 700 tribes from the U.S. & Canada.

Kodak Albuquerque International Balloon Fiesta

Albuquerque, New Mexico
October 4–12, 2003
www.balloonfiesta.com
505-821-1000

Mass ascensions, over 850 balloons, nighttime balloon glows, competitions.

National Fiery Foods and Barbecue Show

Featured on page 25

Albuquerque, New Mexico
March 7–9, 2003
www.fiery-foods.com/ffshow
505-873-8680

Hot & spicy foods tradeshow, tastings, sales, cookbook signings, demos.

SWAIA Santa Fe Indian Market

Santa Fe, New Mexico
August 22–24, 2003
www.swaia.org
505-983-5220

Meet Indian artists, learn about contemporary Indian arts & cultures.

Oregon

Eugene Celebration

Eugene, Oregon
September 19–21, 2003
www.eugenecelebration.com
541-681-4108

Community street party, entertainment, art shows, races, parades.

Boatnik

Grants Pass, Oregon
May 22–26, 2003
www.boatnik.com
541-474-2361

Lots of boat racing on the Rogue River & other festival events.

Britt Festival Classical Series

Jacksonville, Oregon
August 1–16, 2003
www.brittfest.org
800-882-7488

A thoroughly enjoyable musical experience dedicated to classical music concerts.

Cider Season Celebration

Bend, Oregon
September 27, 2003
www.highdesert.org
541-382-4754

Help make apple cider & drink it! Other early-American, hands-on activities.

Fiesta Cinco de Mayo

Portland, Oregon
May 1–4, 2003
www.cincodemayo.org
503-222-9807

Family-oriented, multi-cultural festival celebrating Hispanic heritage.

Mt. Angel Oktoberfest

Mt. Angel, Oregon
September 11–14, 2003

Food chalets laden with rich, delicious Bavarian treats; arts & crafts, activities

Oregon Brewers Festival

Portland, Oregon
July 25–27, 2003
www.oregonbrewfest.com
503-778-5917

Gathering of independent brewers features the finest craft beers.

Oregon Shakespeare Festival

Ashland, Oregon
February 21 – November 2, 2003

Plays performed indoors & out, favorites, rare masterpieces & new plays.

Portland Rose Festival

Portland, Oregon
May 29 – June 29, 2003
www.rosefestival.org
503-227-2681

Celebrate the City of Roses with exciting events & entertainment for all ages.

Rhododendron Festival

Florence, Oregon
May 16–18, 2003
www.florencechamber.com
541-997-3128 or 800-524-4864

Rhododendron blooms, Grand Floral parade, arts & crafts, vendors.

Sandy Mountain Festival

Sandy, Oregon
July 12–13, 2003
www.sandymountainfestival.org
503-668-5900

Stroll wooded paths through a juried fine art show, tunes on the main stage.

Tigard Festival of Balloons

Tigard, Oregon
June 13–15, 2003
www.ci.tigard.or.us
503-639-4171

Join in on the spectacular sight of launchings & night glows at Cook Park!

Waterfront Blues Festival

Portland, Oregon
July 2–6, 2003
www.waterfrontbluesfest.com
503-282-0555

Non-stop blues overlooking the Willamette River, workshops & films.

Yoshida's Sand In the City

Portland, Oregon
July 11–13, 2003
www.kobap.org/kob
503-736-3200

Annual sand sculpture contest in Portland's Pioneer Courthouse Square.

Utah

Cadillac Park City Art Festival

Park City, Utah
August 2–3, 2003
www.kimball-art.org
435-649-8882

Open air market of fine arts, a favorite with both art collectors & browsers.

Sundance Film Festival

Park City, Utah
January 16–26, 2003
www.sundance.org
801-328-3456

Showcase for American independent films, panel discussions & special events.

Utah Arts Festival

Featured on page 36

Salt Lake City, Utah
June 19–22, 2003
www.uaf.org
801-322-2428

Artists Marketplace, almost every genre of music, International Street Theater.

Utah Shakespearean Festival

Cedar City, Utah
June 19 – October 18, 2003
www.bard.org
800-752-9849

Live Shakespearean & modern classic theatre, seminars, a Royal Feaste, tours.

Washington

A Taste of Edmonds

Edmonds, Washington
August 8–10, 2003
www.edmondswa.com/events/taste
425-670-9112

Food booths, live entertainment, beer garden, kids' activities, arts, crafts.

Allegro's Royal Fireworks Festival and Concert

Spokane, Washington
July 26–27, 2003
www.allegrobaroque.org
800-248-3230

Baroque-period music, dance, theatre, visual arts, living history, historical fun.

Anacortes Arts Festival

Anacortes, Washington
August 1–3, 2003
www.AnacortesArtsFestival.com
360 293-6211

Arts & food vendors, entertainment, working artist area, Art at the Port.

Bellevue Art Museum Fair

Bellevue, Washington
July 25–27, 2003
www.bellevueart.org/fair
425-519-0742

Visual fine arts festival, juried artists; visual art exhibitions, Film & Video.

Best of the Northwest

Featured on page 37

Multiple dates
Seattle, Washington
Portland, Oregon
www.bestnwcrafts.com
360-221-8131

Artists & musicians treat art enthusiasts to high-quality & unique arts & crafts.

Blackberry Festival

Bermerton, Washington
August 30–31, 2003
www.blackberryfestival.org
360-377-3041

Childrens area, live music, car show, fly-in, fun run, bike ride, food & crafts.

Bloomsday Run

Spokane, Washington
May 2–4, 2003
www.bloomsdayrun.com
509-838-1579

Popular 12K event, Trade Show, food, music, entertainment after the run.

Bumbershoot The Seattle Arts Festival

Seattle, Washington
August 20 – September 2, 2003
www.onereel.org
206-281-7788

Exciting array of music, crafts, imports, artists in action, film festival, comedy.

Chewelah Chataqua

Chewelah, Washington
July 11–13, 2003
www.chewelah.org/chataqua
509-935-8991

Arts & crafts, entertainment, food, square dance, parade, tournaments.

Daffodil Festival

Tacoma, Washington
April 11–13, 2003
www.daffodilfestival.net
253-627-6176

Annual event ends in Grand Floral Parade through Pierce County cities.

Emerald Queen Casino Taste of Tacoma

Tacoma, Washington
June 27–29, 2003
www.tasteoftacoma.com
425-283-5050

The Ultimate Family Picnic: restaurants, entertainment, juried arts & crafts.

Everett Salty Sea Days and Blues By The Bay

Everett, Washington
June 5–8, 2003
www.saltyseadays.org
425-339-0113

Funtastic Shows Carnival, food booths on the waterfront, Limited Hydro races.

Fremont Summer Solstice Parade and Fair

Seattle, Washington
June 21–22, 2003
www.fremontfair.com
206-726-2623

Artistic vision & playful spirit: people-powered parade & Fremont Fair.

General Motors Cup at Seafair

Seattle, Washington
August 1–3, 2003
www.seafair.com
206-728-0123

Unlimited hydroplanes sporting spectacle, logboom for boats, GM car show.

IKEA Renton River Days

Renton, Washington
July 22–27, 2003
www.RentonRiverDays.org
425-430-6528

variety stage entertainment: magicians, dancers, musicians; recreational events.

Issaquah Salmon Days Festival

Issaquah, Washington
October 4–5, 2003
www.salmondays.org
206-270-2532

Returning salmon are cause for celebration with non-stop FREE activities.

Kla Ha Ya Days Festival

Snohomish, Washington
July 18–20, 2003
www.klahayadays.com
360-568-7076

Running frog jump contest, hot air balloons, fireworks, parade, car show.

Northwest Folklife Festival

Seattle, Washington
May 23–26, 2003
www.nwfolklife.org
206-684-7300

Multi-faceted interpretive cultural demonstrations, music, dance, exhibits.

Olympia Harbor Days Tugboat Festival and Races

Olympia, Washington
August 29–31, 2003
www.harbordays.com
800-788-8847

Tugboat races, maritime arts & crafts, tugboat tours, antique tugboats.

QFC Bite of Seattle

Seattle, Washington
July 18–20, 2003
www.biteofseattle.com
425-283-5050

Fine local restaurants, wines & microbrews, entertainment, chefs' demos.

Royal Fireworks Festival and Concert

Spokane, Washington
July 26–27, 2003
www.allegrobaroque.org
747-3230 or 800-248-3230

Baroque-period arts festival of music, theatre, dance, visual arts, historical fun.

Seafair

Seattle, Washington
July 4 – August 3, 2003
www.seafair.com
206-728-0123

Torchlight Parade, Unlimited Hydroplane Races, Milk Carton Derby.

Seattle International Children's Festival

Seattle, Washington
May 12–20, 2003
www.seattleinternational.org
206-684-7346

Theater, music, dance, acrobatics; artists from other cultures of the world.

Seattle International Film Festival

Seattle, Washington
May 22 – June 15, 2003
www.seattlefilm.com
206-324-9996

Showcases films in all formats from all around the world, discussion forums.

Skagit Valley Tulip Festival

Mount Vernon, Washington
April 1–30, 2003
www.tulipfestival.org
360-428-5959

Celebrates the beauty of the tulips as they bloom, over 700 acres of tulips.

Spokane Lilac Festival

Spokane, Washington
May 10–18, 2003
www.lilacfestival.org
509-326-3339

Lilacs bloom in Manito Park, Armed Forces Torchlight Parade, Lilac Queen.

Summerfest! 2003

Kirkland, Washington
July 11–13, 2003
www.kirklandartscenter.org
425-822-7161

Artists, performers & craftspeople from around the Northwest.

Tacoma Freedom Fair and Airshow

Tacoma, Washington
July 4, 2003
www.FreedomFair.com
253-756-9808

Aviation acts, food booths, arts & crafts in parks on the bay, fireworks.

Taste! Kirkland

Kirkland, Washington
September 13–14, 2003
www.tastekirkland.com
425-822-7066

Marina Park hosts food court, public market, arts & crafts, entertainment.

University of Washington Summer Arts Festival

Featured on page 38

July 16–19, 2003
Seattle, Washington
www.summerartsfest.org
206-685-6696

Celebration of the arts, features performances, exhibits, lectures, workshops

Viking Fest

Poulsbo, Washington
May 16–18, 2003
VikingFest.org
360-779-3378

Celebrate Norwegian Independence Day.

Village Lighting Festival

Leavenworth, Washington
December 6–20, 2003
www.leavenworth.org
509-548-5807

Food & roasting chestnuts, sleigh rides, singing & the village lighting.

Walla Walla Fair and Frontier Days

Walla Walla, Washington
August 27 – September 1, 2003

Concert, demo derby, PRCA rodeo, carnival, midway, horse racing, exhibits.

Washington State Apple Blossom Festival

Wenatchee, Washington
Aril 24 – May 4, 2003
www.appleblossom.org
509-662-3616

Parades, juried art exhibit, car shows, square dances, the Apple Blossom Run.

Washington State International Kite Festival

Featured on page 39

Long Beach, Washington
August 18–25, 2003
www.kitefestival.com
800-451-2542

Kites & competitions, display of Trains & Arches, family fun on the beach.

Wyoming

Beartrap Summer Festival

Casper, Wyoming
July 19–20, 2003
www.beatrapfestival.com
307-235-9325

Bluegrass & Blues atop Casper Mountain, vendors, fresh air, pines!

Grand Teton Music Festival–Winter Series

Jackson Hole, Wyoming
September 7, 2002 – March 15, 2003
www.gtmf.org
307-733-3050

Classical music concerts, Music Appreciation Lectures–casual & informative.

Illinois

Apple 'n' Pork Festival

Clinton, Illinois
September 26–28, 2003
chmoore@davesworld.net
217-935-6066

Mouth-watering apple & pork, flea market, mansion tours, strolling singers.

Bagelfest

Featured on page 13
Mattoon, Illinois
July 25–27, 2003
www.villageprofile.com/illinois/mattoon
217-235-5661

Big Bagel Breakfast, entertainment, Bagel Beauties, arts & crafts, street dance.

Balloon Classic Illinois

Danville, Illinois
June 6–8, 2003
www.balloonclassic.org
800-383-4386

Five balloon races, Balloon Glo, carnival, family-land, fireworks.

Chicago Air and Water Show

Chicago, Illinois
August 16–17, 2003
www.cityofchicago.org/SpecialEvents/Festivals.html
312-744-3370

Civilian & U.S. military aircraft & watercraft exhibitions on Chicago's lakefront.

Chicago Blues Festival

Chicago, Illinois
May 29–June 1, 2003
www.cityofchicago.org
312-744-3370

All-star lineups celebrate the blues in the city that helped make them famous.

Chicago Country Music Festival

Chicago, Illinois
June 28–29, 2003
www.cityofchicago.org
312-744-3370

Bluegrass, new country, western swing & Cajun flows from outdoor stages.

Chicago Gospel Festival

Chicago, Illinois
June 6–8, 2003
www.cityofchicago.org
312-744-3370

Featuring inspirational music from outstanding gospel artists.

Chicago Humanities Festival

Featured on page 14
Chicago, Illinois
October 25 – November 9, 2003
www.chfestival.org
312-494-9509

Discover the rich & vital role the humanities play in our daily lives.

Chicago Jazz Festival

Chicago, Illinois
August 29–31, 2003
www.cityofchicago.org/specialevents
312-744-3370

Great local, national & international jazz performers, art fare, education.

Decatur Celebration

Decatur, Illinois
August 1–3, 2003
www.decaturcelebration.com
217-423-4222

Stage & street attractions, arts & crafts, one-of-a-kind foods, entertainment.

Frankfort Fall Festival

Frankfort, Illinois
August 30 – September 1, 2003
www.frankfortchamber.com
815-469-3356

Juried arts & crafts, Entertainment Tent, carnival, community parade.

Gold Coast Art Fair

Chicago, Illinois
August 8–10, 2003
www.amdurproductions.com/goldcoast
312-787-2677

Considered the "Grand Daddy" of most art fairs & festivals.

Harvard Milk Days Festival

Harvard, Illinois
June 6–8, 2003
www.milkdays.com
815-943-4614

Salute to the dairy farmer includes parades, farm tours, carnival, fireworks.

Illinois Snow Sculpting Competition

Rockford, Illinois
January 14–17, 2004
snowsculpting.org
815-987-8800

Teams of artists carve works of frozen art from huge blocks of snow.

Last Fling

Naperville, Illinois
August 29 – September 1, 2003
www.naperjaycees.org/fling.html
630-961-4143

Final chance for everyone to let loose, have fun & end summer with a bang!

Marigold Festival

Pekin, Illinois
September 6–8, 2003
www.pekin.net/marigold_festival
309-346-2106

Miss Marigold, Medallion Hunt, art in the park, food, tournaments & contests.

Moline Riverfest

Moline, Illinois
June 27–29, 2003
www.qconline.com/riverfest
309-797-0462

Enjoy this family festival on the banks of the Mississippi River.

On the Waterfront Festival

Rockford, Illinois
August 28–31, 2003
www.onthewaterfront.com
815-964-4388

Music festival congregates along both sides of the Rock River.

Ravinia Festival

Highland Park, Illinois
June 6 – September 13, 2003
www.ravinia.org
847-266-5100

North America's oldest music festival, presents the world's biggest music stars.

St. Charles Scarecrow Festival

St. Charles, Illinois
October 10–12, 2003
www.scarecrowfest.com
630-3776161

Family fun, a popular vote scarecrow competition & make-your-own venue.

Taste of Chicago

Chicago, Illinois
June 27 – July 6, 2003
www.cityofchicago.org/specialevents
312-744-3370

Famous food festival features live music all day & headliners every evening.

Viva! Chicago Latin Music Festival

Chicago, Illinois
August 23–24, 2003
www.cityofchicago.org
312-744-3370

Celebrates Latin culture, food, music & traditions of the Latino Community.

Indiana

500 Festival

Indianapolis, Indiana
May 4–25, 2003
www.500festival.com
800-638-4296

Indianapolis 500 race and a showcase of cultural, educational & social events.

Amish Acres Arts and Crafts Festival

Nappanee, Indiana
August 7–10, 2003
amishacres.com/aa_arts_crafts_festival
574-773-4188 x215

Juried artists around the pond, bluegrass & country, dancers, storytellers.

Auburn Cord Duesenberg Festival

Auburn, Indiana
August 27 – September 1, 2003
acdfestival.org
260-925-3600

World's Greatest Classic Car Show & Celebration.

Berne Swiss Days

Berne, Indiana
July 24–26, 2003
www.bernein.com
260-589-8080

Swiss heritage of music, polka, quilts, arts & crafts, factory tours, sidewalk sale.

Bill Monroe Bean Blossom Bluegrass Festival

Bean Blossom, Indiana
June 15–22, 2003
www.beanblossom.com
800-414-4677

Top bluegrass talent, virtuoso musicians, workshops, competitions.

Feast of the Hunters' Moon

West Lafayette, Indiana
September 13–14, 2003
www.tcha.mus.in.us
765-476-8411

Native American & European performances, 1700s military & lifestyle demos.

Indy Jazz Fest

Indianapolis, Indiana
June 13–15, 2003
www.indyjazzfest.org
800-983-4639

Local, national, & international performers, jazz, blues, zydeco, gospel.

Johnny Appleseed Festival

Fort Wayne, Indiana
September 20–21, 2003
www.johnnyappleseedfest.com
219-427-6003

Pioneer spirit of Johnny Appleseed, crafts, music, period entertainers.

Madison Chautauqua

Madsion, Indiana
September 27–28, 2003
www.madisonchautauqua.com
800-559-2956

Juried fine arts & crafts, continuous entertainment, Foodfest, kids activities.

Marshall County Blueberry Festival

Plymouth, Indiana
August 30 – September 2, 2003
blueberryfestival.org
888-936-5020

Luscious blueberry treats, 15K run, hot air balloons, crafts, car show, sports.

Valparaiso Popcorn Festival

Valparaiso, Indiana
September 6–9, 2003
www.popcornfest.org
219-464-8332

Honors Orville Redenbacher, Popcorn Queen & other contests, Talent Show.

New Haven Canal Days Festival

New Haven, Indiana
June 3–7, 2003
nhfestival@aol.com
260-749-2972

Amusement rides, car cruise, Kids' Day, fishing derby, 5 & 10K Run, parade.

West Side Nut Club Fall Festival

Evansville, Indiana
October 6–11, 2003
www.nutclub.org
812-464-8347

Street festival, two midways, assortment of foods, nightly entertainment.

Old Settlers Days

Columbia City, Indiana
June 17–21, 2003
chamber@columbiacity.org
219-248-8131

Bands on the courthouse square, carnival, games, art & flower shows.

Wizard of Oz Festival

Chesterton, Indiana
September 19–20, 2003
wpl.lib.in.us/chamber/Oz
219-926-5513

Meet the original Munchkins, Dorothy & her friends, everything Oz.

Parke County Covered Bridge Festival

Rockville, Indiana
October 10–19, 2003
www.coveredbridges.com
765-569-5226

Guided bus tours to rural bridges, homemade foods, Farmers' Market.

Iowa

Des Moines Arts Festival

Des Moines, Iowa
June 27–29, 2003
www.desmoinesartsfestival.org
515-288-2258

Enjoy original artwork, live entertainment, children's arts activities, fireworks.

DubuqueFest

Dubuque, Iowa
May 16–18, 2003
dubuquearts@yahoo.com
563-588-4400

Arts & crafts, Old House Tour, kids' art tent, poetry reading, live music & dance.

Cedar Rapids Freedom Festival

Featured on page 15

Cedar Rapids, Iowa
June 26 – July 6, 2003
www.freedomfestival.com
319-365-8313

Patriotic celebration offering concerts, cardboard boat regatta, fireworks.

Iowa City Jazz Festival

Iowa City, Iowa
July 4–6, 2003
www.iowacityjazzfestival.com
319-358-9346

National & international acts, jazz workshops along with food & fun!

Mississippi Valley Blues Festival

Davenport, Iowa
July 3–5, 2003
www.mvbs.org
563-322-5837

All-in-one street festival, park picnic, history lesson & live outdoor concert.

National Balloon Classic

Indianola, Iowa
August 1–9, 2003
www.nationalballoonclassic.com
800-359-4692

Enjoy a spectator-oriented balloon extravaganza, fly both morning & evening.

National Hobo Convention

Britt, Iowa
August 8–10, 2003
515-843-3867

Hobo Jungle, Hobo Museum, storytelling, traditional mulligan stew.

National Old Time Country & Bluegrass Festival & Contest

Missouri Valley, Iowa
August 25–31, 2003
www.oldtimemusic.bigstep.com
712-762-4363

Traditional, acoustic, old-time Americana music. Come join the fun!

Sturgis Falls Celebration

Cedar Falls, Iowa
June 27–29, 2003
www.sturgisfalls.org
319-277-0996

Sounds of jazz, country, rock & roll, blues, street fair, carnival, talent contest.

The Taste of Cedar Rapids

Cedar Rapids, Iowa
August 30 – September 1, 2003
www.tasteofcedarrapids.com
319-398-0449

Outstanding musical acts, fine food, interactive fun, nightly fireworks.

Kansas

Arkalalah

Arkansas City, Kansas
October 18–25, 2003
www.arkcityks.org/arkalah.html
620-442-6077

Held annually since 1928, parades, carnival, Queen Alalah coronation, concert.

Country Stampede

Manhattan, Kansas
June 26–29, 2003
www.countrystampede.com
800-795-8091

Today's hottest country stars under the stars at Tuttle Creek State Park.

Dodge City Days

Dodge City, Kansas
July 25 – August 3, 2003
www.dodgecitydays.com
620-227-3119

Country music concert, rodeo, crafts, barbecue contest, Western Parade.

Hillsboro Arts and Crafts Fair

Hillsboro, Kansas
September 20, 2003
home.southwind.net
620-947-3506

Crafts & fine arts, ethnic foods, entertainment, a shoppers paradise!

Kansas City Renaissance Festival

Bonner Springs, Kansas
August 30 – October 13, 2003
www.kcrenfest.com
800-373-0357

Harvest Faire includes jugglers, jousting, jesters, minstrels, food fit for a king.

Lenexa Barbeque Battle and Kansas State Championship

Lenexa, Kansas
June 28, 2003
913-541-8592

Children's activities, live music, & of course, barbeque, barbeque & barbeque!

Little Balkans Days

Pittsburg, Kansas
August 28 – September 1, 2003
morningsun.net
620-231-1000

Celebrating the coal mining heritage & lifestyle, tournaments, car show, dances.

Prairie Winds Kite Festival

Kansas City, Kansas
May 16–18, 2003
www.windwizards.com/windwizards
913-856-0145

Celebrates the free-spirited kite; competitions, demos, activities for everyone.

Wichita River Festival

Wichita, Kansas
May 9–17, 2003
wichitafestivals.com
316-267-2817

Concerts, ice cream social, kite fest, fun runs, art & book fair, food, on the river.

Michigan

African World Festival

Detroit, Michigan
August 15–17, 2003
maah-detroit.org
313-494-5800

Music, lectures, film, artists' market, family activities on the riverfront.

Ann Arbor Art Fairs

Ann Arbor, Michigan
July 16–19, 2003
www.annarbor.org
800-888-9487

Three separate fairs of juried art, each with its own flavor & focus.

Ann Arbor Street Art Fair

Ann Arbor, Michigan
July 16–19, 2003
www.artfair.org
734-994-5260

The original fair in Ann Arbor, juried artists, art activities, street performances.

Comerica TasteFest

Detroit, Michigan
July 2–6, 2003
www.comnet.org/tastefest
313-872-0188

Outdoor culinary festival features food from area restaurants, entertainment.

Festival of the Arts

Grand Rapids, Michigan
June 6–8, 2003
www.festivalofthearts.org
616-459-1300

The arts come alive with singers, dancers, actors, visual artists, art activities.

Ford Detroit International Jazz Festival

Detroit, Michigan
August 29 – September 1, 2003
www.detroitjazzfest.com
313-963-7622

Over one hundred open-air concerts. Free.

Great Lakes Folk Festival

East Lansing, Michigan
August 8–10, 2003
www.greatlakesfolkfest.net
301-565-0654
Putting the arts of many nations, races & languages on an equal footing.

Michigan Renaissance Festival

Holly, Michigan
August 16 – September 28, 2003
www.michrenfest.com
800-601-4848
Revelry & adventure you won't soon forget. The excitement doesn't let up!

Muskegon Summer Celebration

Featured on page 20
Muskegon, Michigan
June 26 – July 6, 2003
www.summercelebration.com
231-722-6520
National recording artists, midway, street fair, parade, juried fine arts, crafts.

National Cherry Festival

Traverse City, Michigan
July 5–12, 2003
www.cherryfestival.org
231-947-4230
Air shows, parades, music concerts, arts & crafts, sporting events.

Peach Festival

Romeo, Michigan
August 28 – September 1, 2003
www.mipeachfest.com
810-336-0759
Vegas games, live music, horseback riding, Fly In & Pancake breakfast.

Plymouth International Ice Sculpture Spectacular

Plymouth, Michigan
January 15–20, 2003
www.wattsupinc.com
734-459-6969
Professionals, amateurs, students transform block ice into dazzling art.

Team U.S. National Hot-Air Balloon Championship and Air Show

Battle Creek, Michigan
July 1–6, 2003
www.bcballoons.com
616-962-0592
Air shows & displays, military demos, fireworks, arts & crafts, flea market.

Tulip Time Festival

Holland, Michigan
May 3–10, 2003
www.tuliptime.org
800-822-2770
Celebrate tulips & Dutch heritage, themed parades, Klompen dancing.

Minnesota

Bayfront Blues Festival

Duluth, Minnesota
August 8–10, 2003
www.bayfrontblues.com
715-394-6831

Top name talent, Blues cruise, yearly Block Party.

Duluth Air & Aviation Expo 2003

Duluth, Minnesota
September 20–21, 2003
www.duluthairshow.com
218-628-9996

Come for the weekend & enjoy Minnesota's largest Airshow!

Festival of Nations

St. Paul, Minnesota
May 1–4, 2003
www.festivalofnations.com
612-647-0191

Ethnic groups & traditions, cultural exhibits, folk art demonstrations.

Little Falls Arts and Crafts Fair

Little Falls, Minnesota
September 6–7, 2003
www.littlefallsmnchamber.com
320-632-5155

Nearly every type of craft or art work is sold, some demonstrations.

Metris Uptown Art Fair

Minneapolis, Minnesota
August 1–3, 2003
www.uptownminneapolis.com
612-823-4581

Arts & crafts in painting, photography, sculpture, jewelry, ceramics, fiber.

Minnesota Renaissance Festival

Shakopee, Minnesota
August 16 – September 28, 2003
www.renaissancefest.com
800-966-8215

Arts & crafts, games, armored jousting, fire eaters, comedy, magic, music.

St. Paul Winter Carnival

St. Paul, Minnesota
January 24 – February 2, 2003
www.winter-carnival.com
651-223-4710

Winter fun, Giant Snow Slide, snow & ice sculptures, snow sports.

Taste of Minnesota

St. Paul, Minnesota
July 3–7, 2003
www.tasteofmn.org
651-772-9980

Delicious food from local restaurants, entertainment, marketplace, Kidzone.

TCF Holidazzle Parade

Minneapolis, Minnesota
November 28 – December 28, 2003
www.tcfholidazzle.com
612-376-7669

Dazzling lights & festive floats celebrate the joy & wonder of the season.

Twin Cities Ribfest

Minneapolis, Minnesota
July 23–27, 2003
www.ribamerica.com
612-673-1300

Nation's finest ribrateurs cook-off. The food is sizzlin' & the tunes are hot.

Missouri

Fair Saint Louis

St. Louis, Missouri
July 3–5, 2003

Two air shows each day, spectacular fireworks, educational exhibits, sports.

Festival of American Music & Craftsmanship

Featured on page 21

Branson, Missouri
September 4 – October 25, 2003
www.silverdollarcity.com
800-952-6626

Unique crafts–from carving to coppersmithing–bluegrass, gospel & country.

Festival of the Little Hills

St. Charles, Missouri
August 15–17, 2003
www.historicstcharles.com
800-366-2427

Activities include demonstrations by craftspeople & artisans.

Kansas City Spirit Festival

Kansas City, Missouri
July 3–5, 2003
www.spiritfest.org
816-221-4444

Blues, jazz, country, Christian, folk, reggae & rock, carnival, activities, arts.

Munys Summer Season

St. Louis, Missouri
June 14 – August 10, 2003
www.muny.com
314-361-1900

Broadway-style shows presented in outdoor musical theater.

National Kid's Fest at Silver Dollar City

Featured on page 21

Branson, Missouri
May 31 – August 24, 2003
www.silverdollarcity.com
800-952-6626

Plenty of hands-on fun, activities, games & entertainment for kids.

Plaza Art Fair

Kansas City, Missouri
September 19–21, 2003
www.countryclubplaza.com
816-753-0100

Artwork, music & fine food in the Plaza's classic Spanish architecture.

Route 66 Music Festival

Joplin, Missouri
July 17–19, 2003
www.route66musicfestival.com
4176246444

Classic rock, pop & country music. Food, retail vendors & exhibitors.

Santa-Cali-Gon Days Festival

Independence, Missouri
August 29 – September 1, 2003
santacaligon.com
816-252-4745

Juried arts & crafts show, national country music artists, carnival rides.

St. Charles Christmas Traditions

St. Charles, Missouri
November 28 – December 21, 2003
www.stcharleschristmas.com
800-366-2427

Christmas customs & Santas from around the world, community events.

St. Louis Rib America Festival

St. Louis, Missouri
May 22–25, 2003

Bring a hearty appetite–barbecue secrets & blue ribbon winners showcased.

Tom Sawyer Days and National Fence Painting Contest

Hannibal, Missouri
July 2–5, 2003
www.hannibaljaycees.org
(866) 263-4825

Highlight is the National Fence Painting Contest judged on speed & accuracy.

World-Fest at Silver Dollar City

Featured on page 21

Branson, Missouri
April 11 – May 18, 2003
www.silverdollarcity.com
800-952-6626

Performers bring world-wide music, dance, costumes & culture.

Nebraska

Comstock Rock

Comstock, Nebraska
July 18–20, 2003
www.comstockrock.com
308 728 3113
Unique combination of Rock music, windmills, power parachutes, dancing.

Comstock Windmill Festival

Comstock, Nebraska
June 12–15, 2003
www.comstockrock.com
308 728 3113
Attractions include windmills, country music, hot-air balloon rides, fireworks.

July Jamm

Lincoln, Nebraska
July 25–27, 2003
www.julyjamm.org
402-434-6900
Features hot jazz, blues, Cajun, reggae & Latin musicians.

Nebraskaland Days

North Platte, Nebraska
June 13–24, 2003
www.nebraskalanddays.com
308-532-7939
Buffalo Bill Rodeo with top name cowboys & cowgirls, parades, competitions.

River City Roundup

Omaha, Nebraska
September 20–28, 2003
www.aksarben.org
402-554-9610
Championship rodeos, 4-H livestock expo, trail rides, cook-offs.

North Dakota

Norsk Hostfest

Minot, North Dakota
October 7–11, 2003
www.hostfest.com
701-852-2368
Ethnic festival features Scandinavian delicacies, demonstrations, arts & crafts.

United Tribes International Powwow and Cultural Arts Events

Bismarck, North Dakota
September 4–7, 2003
www.unitedtribespowwow.com
701-255-3285 x293
Cultural pride showcased in drum & dance competitions, pageant, art expo.

Ohio

Big Bear Balloon Festival

Grove City, Ohio
June 20–22, 2003
www.balloonfestival.com
800-468-2479
The magic of hot air balloons, lumberjack shows, high dives, puppet shows.

Bigg's Kids' Fest

Cincinnati, Ohio
May 31–June 1, 2003
www.wvmx.com
513-621-9326
Multiple free activities & shows line the Central Riverfront.

Circleville Pumpkin Show

Circleville, Ohio
October 15–18, 2003
www.pumpkinshow.com
740-474-2828
Everything that can be made out of pumpkins–Pumpkin burgers, anyone?

Columbus Arts Festival

Columbus, Ohio
June 5–8, 2003
www.gcac.org
614-224-2606
Professionally juried show, artists from across North America, art activities.

Columbus Jazz and RibFest

Columbus, Ohio
July 18–21, 2003
www.columbus.org/jazz
614-225-6080
Join us for hot ribs & cool jazz. Free.

Dublin Irish Festival

Dublin, Ohio
August 1–3, 2003
www.dublinirishfestival.org
877-67-47336 or 614-410-4545
Grand Dublin style, marketplace cultural exhibits, wee folk activities.

Festival Latino

Columbus, Ohio
June 20–21, 2003
www.musicintheair.org/festivals
614-645-7995
Presentations & dances to live sounds of Timba, Salsa, Tango, & Conjunto.

Jackson County Apple Festival

Jackson, Ohio
September 16–20, 2003
www.jacksonapplefestival.com
800-522-7564
Mountains of apples & barrels of cider from the orchards set the scene.

Jamboree in the Hills
Morristown, Ohio
July 17–20, 2003
www.jamboreeinthehills.com
800-624-5456

The Superbowl of Country Music festivals. Squirt gun fights break out.

Marion Popcorn Festival
Marion, Ohio
September 4–6, 2003
www.popcornfestival.com
740-387-3378

Food, games, rides & free live entertainment.

MIX 94.1 Kids' Fest
Cincinnati, Ohio
June 7–8, 2003
www.wvmx.com
513-852-1646

Multiple free activities & shows line the Central Riverfront.

National Tractor Pulling Championships
Featured on page 31
Bowling Green, Ohio
August 15–17, 2003
www.pulltown.com
888-385-7855

Tractors of all shapes & sizes compete to see whose rig is strongest & fastest.

Northwest Ohio Rib-Off
Toledo, Ohio
August 7–10, 2003
www.uhs-toledo.org/riboff
419-242-9587

Family picnic rib cook-off, vying for the People's Choice & Golden Rib awards.

Ohio Pumpkin Festival
Barnesville, Ohio
September 25–28, 2003
www.ohighway.com/belmont-county-tourism
740-695-4359

King Pumpkin contest, Queen Pageant, Giant Pumpkin parade, music contests.

Ohio Renaissance Festival
Harveysburg, Ohio
August 23–October 19, 2003
www.renfestival.com
513-897-7000

Visit 16th Century England in this authentic 30-acre English Village.

Ohio Sauerkraut Festival
Waynesville, Ohio
October 11–13, 2003

Arts, crafts & sauerkraut "served every tasty way you can imagine."

Piqua Heritage Festival

Piqua, Ohio
August 30 – September 1, 2003
www.piquaoh.org
937-773-9744

Recreated Native American villages, costumed 1840s pioneers, spelling bees.

Riverfest

Cincinnati, Ohio
August 31, 2003
www.webn.com
513-852-1646

Food & entertainment during the day; spectacular fireworks in the evening,

Tall Stacks 2003

Cincinnati, Ohio
October 15–19, 2003
www.tallstacks.com
866-497-8255

Celebrates the Steamboat Age, riverboat cruises & races, educational exhibits.

Tops Great American Rib Cook-Off

Cleveland, Ohio
May 22–26, 2003
belkinproductions.com/ribcookoff
440-247-2722

Outdoor cookout with national rib-cooking teams competing for prizes.

Troy Strawberry Festival

Troy, Ohio
June 7–8, 2003
www.tdn-net.com/strawberryfest
937-339-7714

Celebrate the sweet, ripe Troy strawberry, arts & crafts, sporting competitions.

Twins Days Festival

Twinsburg, Ohio
August 1–3, 1003
www.twinsdays.org
330-425-3652

Double fun, double takes & double trouble–twins & other multiples.

South Dakota

Black Hills Heritage Festival, Music and Community Celebration

Rapid City, South Dakota
July 3–4, 2003
www.bhheritagefest.com
605-341-5940

Acoustic & concert style entertainment, cultural pavilion, children's activities.

Buffalo Chip Concert Series

Sturgis, South Dakota
August 4–10, 2003
www.buffalochip.com
605-892-2200

The Best Party Anywhere! Concerts, swap meet, vendors, camping.

Corn Palace Festival

Mitchell, South Dakota
August 27 – September 1, 2003
www.cornpalacefestival.com
800-289-7469

Celebrate the corn harvest. Midway, specialty vendors, headline entertainment.

Sioux Falls Jazz and Blues Festival

Sioux Falls, South Dakota
July 18–19, 2003
www.jazzfestsiouxfalls.com
605-335-6101

FREE to the public! Music, food & craft vendors.

Sturgis Rally

Sturgis, South Dakota
August 4–10, 2003
www.sturgishd.com
605-347-6570

Thousands of motorcyclists, the granddaddy of all motorcycle rallies & races.

Wisconsin

Art Fair On the Square

Madison, Wisconsin
July 12–13, 2003
www.madisonartcenter.org
608-257-0158

Artists from the U.S. & abroad show their creations, music, dance & theater.

Artstreet

Green Bay, Wisconsin
August 22–24, 2003
www.newartscouncil.org
920-435-2787

Visual & performing arts, fine arts, ethnic foods, literary arts corner, activities.

Bastille Day

Milwaukee, Wisconsin
July 10–14, 2003
bastille.easttown.com
414-271-7400

Experience Paris: sidewalk cafés, wine bistros, cabaret, fashion shows, parade.

Bristol Renaissance Faire

Kenosha, Wisconsin
June 28 – August 24, 2003
www.recfair.com/bristol
847-395-7773

Join Queen Elizabeth I & her court to enjoy arts & crafts, food, entertainment.

Country Jam USA

Eau Claire, Wisconsin
July 17–19, 2003
www.countryjam.com
800-780-0526

Country music featuring the nation's hottest artists, acres of vendors, food.

EAA AirVenture

Oshkosh, Wisconsin
July 29 – August 4, 2003
convention@eaa.org
920-426-4800

Air shows, museum, exhibitors, forums, children's & evening programs.

German Fest

Milwaukee, Wisconsin
July 25–27, 2003
www.germanfest.com
414-464-9444

America's quintessential German city hosts Oktoberfest in July!

Hodag Country Festival

Rhinelander, Wisconsin
July 10–13, 2003
http://hodag.com
715-369-1300

Top-notch country music, contests, even a Guitar Mass on Sunday.

Indian Summer Festival

Milwaukee, Wisconsin
September 5–7, 2003
www.indiansummer.org
414-774-7119

Competition powwow, American Indian foods, villages, cultural demos.

Kites on Ice

Madison, Wisconsin
February 1–2, 2003

Kiters fly, exhibit, demonstrate, & teach techniques for kiting on the ice.

Mexican Fiesta

Milwaukee, Wisconsin
August 22–24, 2003
www.mexicanfiesta.org
414-383-7066

Great Mexican music, vibrant costumes & dancing, jalapeno-eating contest!

Milwaukee Irish Fest

Milwaukee, Wisconsin
August 14–17, 2003
www.irishfest.com
414-476-3378

Major Irish & Irish American entertainers, sports, drama, contests, marketplace.

Oktoberfest

LaCrosse, Wisconsin
September 26 – October 4, 2003
www.oktoberfestusa.com
608-784-3378

Authentic Old World celebration in German tradition, special events.

Summerfest

Milwaukee, Wisconsin
June 26 – July 6, 2003
www.summerfest.com
800-273-3378

An incredible live music experience: 13 stages on the shores of Lake Michigan.

Warrens Cranberry Festival

Featured on page 40

Warrens, Wisconsin
September 26–28, 2003
www.cranfest.com
608-378-4200

Cranberry Capital of Wisconsin hosts vendors, specialty markets, contests.

Alabama

Arts & Crafts Festival of Fairhope

Fairhope, Alabama
March 14–16, 2003
www.ESchamber.com/arts
251-621-8222

Prestigious juried show includes food & live local entertainment.

BayFest

Mobile, Alabama
October 3–5, 2003
www.bayfest.com
251-208-7835

Outdoor music festival features over 100 acts in all musical genres.

City Stages

Birmingham, Alabama
May 16–18, 2003
www.citystages.org
205-251-1272

Birmingham's World-Class Music Festival.

Jubilee CityFest

Montgomery, Alabama
May 23–25, 2003
www.jubileecityfest.org
334 834-7220

Family weekend festival featuring non-stop entertainment.

Mobile International Festival

Featured on page 3

Mobile, Alabama
November 22, 2003
www.mobileinternationalfestival.org
251-470-7730

Educational & cultural event, booths, hands-on art, entertainment.

National Peanut Festival

Dothan, Alabama
October 31 – November 8, 2003
www.nationalpeanutfestival.com
334-793-4323

Celebrating peanuts & fun in the "Peanut Capitol of the World."

National Shrimp Festival

Gulf Shores, Alabama
October 9–12, 2003
www.nationalshrimpfestival.com
334-968-4237

Salute to the shrimp fishing industry features four days of free family fun.

Panoply Arts Festival

Huntsville, Alabama
April 25–27, 2003
www.panoply.org
256-519-2787

Arts event of top-quality & diverse shows, activities & competition.

W.C. Handy Music Festival

Florence, Alabama
July 27 – August 2, 2003
www.wchandyfest.org
800-472-5897

Celebrates the musical heritage of native W.C. Handy, the father of the blues.

Arkansas

Albert E. Brumley Gospel Sing

Fayetteville, Arkansas
July 30 – August 2, 2003
www.brumleymusic.com
800-435-3725

The undisputed granddaddy of outdoor music festivals.

Bean Fest and Great Championship Outhouse Race

Mountain View, Arkansas
October 24–26, 2003
www.mountainviewcc.org
870-269-8068

An experience derived in the Folk Music Capital of the World.

Dogwood Arts and Crafts Festival

Siloam Springs, Arkansas
April 25–27, 2003
www.siloamchamber.com
501-524-6466

Arts & crafts from around the country, top-notch entertainment.

Fort Smith Regional Airshow

Fort Smith, Arkansas
May 3–4, 2003
dkrutsch@earthlink.net
501-646-1681

Biennial event features demonstrations, rides, simulators & aircraft displays.

Hope Watermelon Festival

Hope, Arkansas
August 7–19, 2003
www.hopemelonfest.com
870-777-3640

Arts & crafts, food, entertainment, & the Watermelon Olympics.

PurpleHull Pea Festival

Emerson, Arkansas
June 27–28, 2003
www.purplehull.com
870-547-2707

Paying homage to this delicacy grown in area gardens, fun races & competitions.

Quadrangle Street Festival

Texarkana, Arkansas
September 6–7, 2003
www.texarkanamuseums.org
903-793-4831

Historic downtown twin city with events on the state line.

Riverfest

Little Rock & North Little Rock, Arkansas
May 23–25, 2003
www.riverfestarkansas.com
501-255-3378

Arkansas' largest & most popular music, arts & food festival.

Smoke on the Water Barbecue and Music Festival

Pine Bluff, Arkansas
September 19–20, 2003
www.smokeonthewaterbbq.com
870.536.8175

Features championship barbecue cook-off, music, arts & crafts, & carnival.

Toad Suck Daze

Conway, Arkansas
May 2–4, 2003
www.toadsuck.org
501-327-7788

Toad Jumps, Toad Suck Daze Melodrama, Toad Store, fun runs & contests.

World's Championship Duck Calling Contest

Stuttgart, Arkansas
November 22–29, 2003
www.stuttgartarkansas.com
870-673-1602

It may be time for turkey, but in Stuttgart they celebrate a different fowl!

Delaware

Dewey Beach Music Festival

Dewey Beach, Delaware
September 25–28, 2003
www.deweybeachfest.com
717-234-4342

Mentoring sessions, industry meet & greets, performance showcases.

Punkin' Chunkin' Contest

Millsboro, Delaware
October 31 – November 2, 2003
www.punkinchunkin.com
302-684-8196

Unlucky pumpkins from homemade launches are smashed to smithereens.

Sea Witch Halloween and Fiddler's Festival

Rehoboth Beach, Delaware
October 24–26, 2003
www.beach-fun.com
800-441-1329

A new Halloween treatment, Hayrides, broom-tossing contest.

Florida

Art Deco Weekend

Miami Beach, Florida
January 17–19, 2003
www.artdecoweekend.com
305-672-2014

Art Deco art, architecture, collectibles, performances, lectures.

Bank of America Viva Broward!

Fort Lauderdale, Florida
October 10–12, 2003
www.vivabroward.com
954-527-5346

Celebrate Hispanic Heritage Month, vendors, Latin foods, Salsa dance lessons.

Bay Area Renaissance Festival

Largo, Florida
March 8 – April 14, 2003
www.renaissancefest.com
800-779-4910

Lively stage & street theatre, human chess matches, minstrels, peasants, jokers.

Beaux Arts Festival of Art

Coral Gables, Florida
January 18–19, 2003
www.pinecrest.com/beaux-arts
305-284-3535

Fine art & crafts, juried exhibitors in a beautiful tropical setting.

Big Squeeze Juice Festival

Palm Bay, Florida
April 4–6, 2003
www.thebigsqueeze.com
800-276-9130

Promoting citrus, exotic fruits & Florida wines, free tastings, concerts, rides.

Biketoberfest

Featured on page 9

Daytona Beach, Florida
October 16–19, 2003
www.biketoberfest.org
866-296-8970

Motorcycle enthusiasts enjoy racing, rides, rallies, bike shows, concerts & fun.

Boggy Bayou Mullet Festival

Niceville, Florida
October 17–19, 2003
www.mulletfestival.com
850-678-1615

Big-name entertainment, arts & crafts, clowns, alligators, mullet munching.

Carnaval Miami (El Festival de la Ocho)

Miami, Florida
March 9, 2003
www.carnaval-miami.org
305-644-8888
Exceptional music & dancing, competitions in Little Havana.

Chasco Fiesta

Featured on page 10
New Port Richey, Florida
March 18–28, 2004
www.chascofiesta.com
727-842-7651
A traditional Native American festival, boat parade, street parade.

Cingular Wireless Winterfest Boat Parade

Fort Lauderdale, Florida
December 13, 2003
www.winterfestparade.com
954-767-0686
Lighted boat parade is a nighttime tradition, brightly lit yachts, singing.

Coconut Grove Arts Festival

Coconut Grove, Florida
February 15–17, 2003
www.coconutgroveartsfest.com
305-447-0401
Arts & crafts, interesting music, food, & above all, people.

Cracker Heritage Festival

Wauchula, Florida
March 8, 2003
www.mainstwauchula.pair.com
873-767-0330
Living history artisans producing homemade tools & crafts, exhibits & shows.

Daytona Harley Davidson Seafood Festival

Daytona Beach, Florida
October 11–13, 2003
www.tomcellie.com
904-248-0580
Family event with rides & games, arts & crafts, music, Police Motorcycle Parade.

Delray Affair

Delray Beach, Florida
April 25–27, 2003
www.delrayaffair.com
561-278-0424
One of the greatest art, craft & entertainment street festivals under the sun!

Delray Beach Garlic Fest

Delray Beach, Florida
November 7–9, 2003
www.dbgarlicfest.com
561-279-0907
Heavenly foods on Gourmet Alley, watch the Garlic Chef competitions.

Downtown Festival and Art Show

Gainesville, Florida
November 8–9, 2003
www.gvlculturalaffairs.org
352-334-5064
Holiday shopping with fine artists, live music, continuous performing arts.

Edison Festival of Light

Fort Myers, Florida
January 25 – February 16, 2003
www.edisonfestival.org
941-334-2999
A light-up block party, children's events, night parade with lit floats.

Everglades Seafood Festival

Everglades City, Florida
February 7–9, 2003
evergladesseafoodfestival.com
941-695-4100
Seafood, gator tails, specialty foods from local Native American tribes.

Fantasy Fest

Key West, Florida
October 17–26, 2003
www.fantasyfest.net
305-296-1817
Goombay Celebration to start, also races, Fat Tuesday, masquerades.

Festival Calle Orange

Orlando, Florida
October 26, 2003
www.Renesproductions.com
407-381-5310
Downtown Orlando hosts this grand celebration of culture.

Fiesta Day

Tampa, Florida
November 29, 2003
www.ybor.org/events
813-248-3712
Historic Ybor City showcases its ethnic roots with this free street festival.

Florida Azalea Festival

Palatka, Forida
March 7–9, 2003
www.flazaleafest.com
904-326-4001
Azaleas in bloom, live entertainment, classic cars, trucks & motorcycles, rides.

Florida Heritage Festival at Bradenton

Bradenton, Florida
March 29 – July 20, 2003
www.desotohq.com
941-747-1998
Fishing tournament, children's parade & party, Easter egg hunt, seafood.

Florida SpringFest

Pensacola, Florida
May 30 – June 1, 2003
www.springfest.net
800-874-1234

Sounds of music & good times with national, regional & local music acts.

Florida Strawberry Festival

Plant City, Florida
February 27 – March 9, 2003
www.flstrawberryfestival.com
813-752-9194

The Winter Strawberry Capital of the World celebrates in grand style.

Gasparilla Festival of the Arts

Tampa, Florida
March 1–2, 2003
www.gasparilla-arts.com
813-876-1747

Artists, local & regional entertainment, hands-on kids' workshop.

Grant Seafood Festival

Grant, Florida
February 22–23, 2003
www.grantseafoodfestival.com
321-723-8687

Delectable clam chowder, linguini & clam sauce, shrimp, scallops, crab, oysters!

Guavaween

Tampa, Florida
October 25, 2003
www.cc-events.org/gw
813-621-7121

Latin-style Halloween celebration with mass mayhem in the streets!

Hialeah Spring Festival

Hialeah, Florida
February 22 – March 2, 2003
www.hialeahchamber.com
350-828-9898

Amusement park, exhibitions, ethnic foods, arts & crafts, exhibits, concerts.

Hispanic Heritage Festival

Featured on page 11

Miami, Florida
October 1–31, 2003
www.hispanicfestival.com
305-461-1014

Outdoor music, sporting events, competitions, Hispanic Gala Ball, golf classic.

Indian River Festival

Titusville, Florida
April 24–27, 2003
www.nbbd.com
321-267-3036

Carnival, commercial & civic displays; raft race, helicopter rides, competitions.

Isle of Eight Flags Shrimp Festival

Fernandina Beach, Florida
May 2–4, 2003
www.shrimpfestival.com
866-426-3542

Juried fine arts & crafts, antiques & collectibles vendors, shrimp specialties.

Junior Orange Bowl International Youth Festival

Coral Gables, Florida
Oct. 11, 2003 – March 14, 2004
www.jrorangebowl.com
305-662-1210

Youth cultural & sporting competitions, golf, tennis, chess, arts, scholastics.

Kumquat Festival

Dade City, Florida
January 25, 2003
www.dadecitychamber.org
352-567-3769

Arts & crafts, buggy rides, farmer's market, vintage fashion show, antique cars.

La Feria De Las Americas

Miami, Florida
October 30 – November 2, 2003
exponica.com
305-227-0123

Cultural art, customs, folklore, music, & flavors of Latin America, experiences.

Lake Worth Street Painting Festival

Lake Worth, Florida
February 22–23, 2003
www.streetpaintingfestival.org
561-582-3729

The streets are an outdoor museum of original art & reproductions.

Longwood Arts and Crafts Festival

Longwood, Florida
November 22–23, 2003
ldennis834@aol.com
407-834-9506

Towering oaks & shady lanes host arts & crafts, good food, & entertainment.

MacDill Air Fest

Tampa, Florida
April 5–6, 2003
www.macdill.af.mil
813-828-4163

The world's finest military & civilian aerial demonstration teams.

Mardi Gras Fiesta Tropicale

Hollywood, Florida
February 21–23, 2003
www.mardigrasfiesta.com
954-926-3377

New Orleans-style music, delicacies, & activities, costume parade & contest.

McDonald's Air and Sea Show

Fort Lauderdale, Florida
April 28 – May 4,2003
www.airseashow.com
954-527-5600 ext. 88

Features thrilling air & sea demos by all five branches of the military.

Miami/Bahamas Goombay Festival

Miami, Florida
June 6–8, 2003
miamigoombay.com
305-372-9966

Black heritage festival features entertainment, vendors.

Miami Beach Festival of the Arts

Miami Beach, Florida
February 8–9, 2003
www.ci.miami-beach.fl.us
305-865-4147

Enriching cultural arts experience with captivating family activities.

Miami Book Fair International

Miami, Florida
November 16–23, 2003
www.literature-awards.com
305-237-3258

Book lovers celebrate the written word, promoting literature & books, reading.

Miami Jazz Festival

Miami, Florida
January 11–12, 2003
www.miamijazzfestival.com
305-858-8545

Live performances of contemporary, traditional, & Latin jazz, blues, gospel.

Naples Downtown Art Festival

Naples, Florida
March 22–23, 2003
howard@artfestival.com
954-472-3755

A juried fine art show is just the beginning, food fest & musical entertainment.

North Florida Fair Outdoor Fine Arts & Crafts Show & Sale

Tallahassee, Florida
October 30 – November 9, 2003
www.northfloridafair.com
850-878-3247

Part of the North Florida Fair, all products are hand-crafted by the artist.

Pensacola JazzFest

Pensacola, Florida
April 5–6, 2003
www.jazzpensacola.com
850-433-8382

Free jazz festival celebrating all styles of jazz.

Port Orange Family Days

Port Orange, Florida
September 27 – October 5, 2003
www.familydays.com
386-267-0540

Business & non-profit exhibits, jet ski rides, karaoke, golf tournament.

Port Orange Festival of Fine Art

Port Orange, Florida
September 13–14, 2003
Poffa2002@aol.com
386-763-0882

Juried fine arts show, prizes awarded in many categories, celebrity hosts.

Ron Jon–Robert August Easter Surfing Festival

Cocoa Beach, Florida
April 17–20, 2003
www.ronjons.com/events
321-799-8888 -1088

Professional & amateur contests, all age groups, surfing clinics, festival village.

San Antonio Rattlesnake Festival

San Antonio, Florida
October 18–19, 2003
www.RattlesnakeFestival.com
352-588-4444

Rattlesnake And Gopher Enthusiasts (RAGE) educational & fun family event.

SeaFest

Port Canaveral, Florida
March 28–30, 2003
www.seafest.com
321-459-2200

Food, sun, & fun; fantastic seafood, ship tours, arts & crafts, games, rides.

Speed Beach Festival

Daytona Beach, Florida
February 14, 2003
www.speedbeach.com

Family Friendly race festivities during the races in Daytona Beach.

Spring Fiesta in the Park

Orlando, Florida
April 5–6, 2003
coxeventsgroup.freehomepage.com
321-281-2085

Outdoor fun, family activities, live entertainment & a wide range of vendors.

Sun 'n' Fun EAA Fly-In

Lakeland, Florida
April 2–8, 2003
www.sun-n-fun.org
863-644-2431

Second largest fly-in world-wide, air–shows, workshops, banquets, movies.

Suncoast Offshore Grand Prix Festival

Sarasota, Florida
June 28 – July 6, 2003
www.suncoastoffshore.org
941-371-2827

Starts with a golf tournament, finishes with Powerboats by the Bay races.

SunFest

West Palm Beach, Florida
April 30 – May 4, 2003
www.sunfest.com
800-SUNFEST

Music, art & waterfront festival features concerts, juried arts, craft marketplace.

Tallahassee Chain of Parks Art Festival

Tallahassee, Florida
April 12–13, 2003
www.lemoyne.org
850-222-8800

Blooming dogwoods & azaleas are backdrop for this juried art show.

Tampa Bay Blues Festival

St. Petersburg, Florida
April 4–6, 2003
www.TampaBayBluesFest.com
727-824-6163

Great music on the fabulous waterfront. Proceeds support three charities.

Winter Park Sidewalk Art Festival

Winter Park, Florida
March 21–23, 2003
www.wpsaf.org
407-672-6390

Juried art show, children's events, Music in the Park free concerts.

Zellwood Sweet Corn Festival

Zellwood, Florida
May 17–18, 2003
www.Zellwoodsweetcornfest.org
407-886-0014

All the locally-grown Zellwood Sweet Corn you can eat, family fun & picnic.

Zora Neale Hurston Festival

Eatonville, Florida
January 24–26, 2003
www.zoranealehurston.cc
321-281-2085

Music, drama, dance, visual arts, folk arts, ethnic cuisine, concerts, & theatre.

Georgia

Atlanta Dogwood Festival

Atlanta, Georgia
April 11–13, 2003
www.dogwood.org
404-329-0501

Outdoor concerts, hot air balloon races, art exhibits, Kid's Village, Eco-village.

Georgia Mountain Fair

Hiawassee, Georgia
August 6–17, 2003
www.georgia-mountain-fair.com
706-896-4191

Pioneer village, clogging, demos of corn milling, soap & hominy making.

Georgia Renaissance Festivals

Fairburn, Georgia
April 26 – June 8, 2003
www.garenfest.com
770-964-8575

Village entertainers, comedic jugglers, rope walking, jousting, marketplace.

Great Atlantic Seafood Festival

Savannah, Georgia
May 2–4, 2003
www.savriverstreet.com
912-234-0295

The very best in food, music & arts on the River.

Labor Day Catfish Festival

Kingsland, Georgia
August 30 – September 1, 2003
www.visitkingsland.com
800-433-0225

Succulent southern fried catfish & Cajun catfish are festival highlights.

International Cherry Blossom Festival

Macon, Georgia
March 21–30, 2003
www.cherryblossom.com
478-751-7429

Festival with the town's 270,000 Yoshino cherry trees in bloom.

Music Midtown, an Atlanta Festival

Atlanta, Georgia
May 2–4, 2003
www.musicmidtown.com
770-MIDTOWN

Energetic people & lots of music provide a unique celebration.

National Black Arts Festival

Atlanta, Georgia
July 18–27, 2003
www.nbaf.org
404-730-7315

Celebrate the achievements & influence of artists of African descent.

Powers Crossroads Country Fair and Arts Festival

Newnan, Georgia
August 30 – September 1, 2003
newnan.com/cowetafestivals
770-253-7011

Juried art show, country, gospel, folk & contemporary music, & clogging.

Riverfest Weekend

Columbus, Georgia
April 25–27, 2003
www.historiccolumbus.com
706-323-7979

Arts, entertainment & festivities galore along the Chattahoochee River.

Stone Mountain Highland Games

Stone Mountain, Georgia
October 18–19, 2003
www.smhg.org
800-317-2006

A regal celebration in the Scottish tradition. Clan competitions, music, dancing.

Sweet Auburn Springfest

Atlanta, Georgia
April 25–27, 2003
www.sweetauburn.com
404-886-0986

Entertainment, international vendors, Business & Technology Expo.

Vidalia Onion Festival

Vidalia, Georgia
April 10–13, 2003
www.vidaliaga.com
912-538-8687

Celebrate the sweet Vidalia Onion, onion eating contests, cooking school.

Yellow Daisy Festival

Stone Mountain, Georgia
September 4–7, 2003
www.stonemountainpark.com
(770) 498-5633

Prestigious traditional craft show, handmade work for appreciation & purchase.

Kentucky

Hillbilly Days

Pikeville, Kentucky
April 18–20, 2003
www.hillbillydays.com
800-844-7453

Celebrate the clear mountain air & warm spring days with music & dancing.

Kentucky Bourbon Festival

Bardstown, Kentucky
September 17–21, 2003
www.kybourbonfestival.com
800-638-4877

Toast to the bourbon industry seeks to enlighten, educate–& maybe intoxicate!

Kentucky Derby Festival

Louisville, Kentucky
April 12 – May 4, 2003
www.kdf.org
502-584-6383

Includes Thunder over Louisville, great balloon race & glow, Pegasus parade.

Marion County Country Ham Days

Lebanon, Kentucky
September 27–28, 2003
www.hamdays.com
270-692-9594

Over 600 hams served, contests, antique gas & steam engines, Climbing Wall.

Trigg County Country Ham Festival

Cadiz, Kentucky
October 10–12, 2003
www.hamfestival.com
888-446-6402

Community food celebration, music, carnival, ingenious food vendors.

W.C. Handy Blues & Barbecue Festival

Henderson, Kentucky
June 11–15, 2003
www.handyblues.org
800-648-3128

Blues-lovers from around the country come for fun & some of the best blues.

World Chicken Festival

London, Kentucky
September 25–28, 2003
www.chickenfestival.com
800-348-0095

The home of Kentucky Fried Chicken pays homage to the formidable fowl.

Louisiana

Cochon de Lait Festival

Mansura, Louisiana
May 8–11, 2003
nickyb@cottonportbank.com
888-488-4513

Cochon de Lait–roast suckling pigs, street dances, pig related contests.

Contraband Days Festival

Lake Charles, Louisiana
April 29 – May 11, 2003
www.contrabanddays.com
337-436-5508

Celebrate the days of pirates & buccaneers who once sailed the area's waters.

Essence Music Festival

New Orleans, Louisiana
July 3–5, 2003
www.essence.com/essence
800-762-9523

Gathering of great African American entertainers, seminars, ethnic market.

Festival International de Louisiane

Lafayette, Louisiana
April 23–27, 2003
www.festivalinternational.com
337-232-8086

French culture & world influences, arts, entertainment, theatre, cuisine.

Festivals Acadiens

Lafayette, Louisiana
September 19–20, 2003
www.lafayettetravel.com/events
800-346-1958

Celebrate the upbeat rhythm of Cajun life in dance, music, crafts, cuisine.

French Quarter Festival

Featured on page 16

New Orleans, Louisiana
April 10–13, 2003
www.fqfi.com
504-522-5730

Local music, New Orleans cuisine, Battle of Jazz Bands, patio tours, fireworks.

Gumbo Festival

Bridge City, Louisiana
October 10–12, 2003
www.hgaparish.org
504-436-4712

The best spicy seafood & gumbo, 5K race, dances, contest.

Mudbug Madness

Shreveport, Louisiana
May 22–25, 2003
www.mudbugmadness.com
318-222-7403

Cajun music & food; Cajun–Zydeco musicians, fried alligator, gumbo.

Natchitoches Christmas Festival

Natchitoches, Louisiana
December 5–6, 2003
www.christmasfestival.com
318-352-6894

Celebrate the season in the oldest settlement in the Louisiana Purchase.

New Orleans Jazz and Heritage Festival

New Orleans, Louisiana
April 24 – May 4, 2003
www.nojazzfest.com
504-941-5100

The American music lovers' rendezvous offering music & culture galore.

Red River Revel Arts Festival

Featured on page 17

Shreveport, Louisiana
October 4–11, 2003
www.redriverrevel.com
318-424-4000

Dedicated to the finest in visual & performing arts & a celebration of creativity.

Satchmo SummerFest

Featured on page 18

New Orleans, Louisiana
July 31 – August 4, 2003
www.fqfi.org
504-522-5730

Finest jazz musicians, seminars on history, conference, jazz mass, parade.

Maryland

Artscape

Baltimore, Maryland
July 25–27, 2003
www.artscape.org
410-752-8632

Artisans, crafters, exhibitors, headliners, performing & culinary arts.

Capital Jazz Fest

Largo, Maryland
June 6–8, 2003
www.capitaljazz.com/jazzfest
301-218-0404

Contemporary jazz artists, unique crafts, ethnic & exotic foods.

Catoctin Color Fest Arts and Crafts Show

Thurmont, Maryland
October 11–12, 2003
www.colorfest.org
301-271-4432

Live music, food, over 360 arts & crafts booths.

Fell's Point Fun Festival

Baltimore, Maryland
October 4–5, 2003
www.preservationsociety.com
410-675-6756

Arts & crafts, flea market, four stages, family & children's areas, beer gardens.

German Festival

Baltimore, Maryland
August 15–17, 2003
www.md-germans.org
410-522-4144

Lively entertainment & authentic German crafts, food & beer, music, dance.

Maryland Renaissance Festival

Crownsville, Maryland
August 23 – October 19, 2003
www.rennfest.com/mrf
410-266-7304

Join the magical world of a 16th-century English festival with Henry VIII.

Maryland Sheep and Wool Festival

West Friendship, Maryland
May 3–4, 2003
sheepandwool.org
410-531-3647

Discover the beauty of sheep, warmth of wool, delicious taste of lamb.

Sharpsburg Heritage Festival

Sharpsburg, Maryland
September 12–14, 2003
www.sharpsburgheritagefestival.org
800-228-7829

Offers visitors a glimpse of what life was like in Sharpsburg's earliest days.

Sunfest

Ocean City, Maryland
September 18–21, 2003
www.ococean.com
800-626-2326

Treasure hunts on the beach, sand sculpting competitions, surf fishing.

Mississippi

HUBfest

Hattiesburg, Mississippi
October 11, 2003
www.theADP.com
800-238-4288

A Southern Celebration with 5 K Run, Pet Walk, crafters, food, entertainment.

Jubilee Jam

Jackson, Mississippi
May 16–18, 2003
www.jubileejam.com
601-355-3378

Downtown festival celebrates state's arts, music, & performers.

Mississippi Coast Fair and Carnival

Biloxi, Mississippi
June 5–15, 2003
www.mscoastcoliseum.com
228-594-3700

Old-fashioned midway, games, contests, parades, & music of all kinds.

Thunder on Water

Grenada, Mississippi
June 13–15, 2003
thunderonwater.com
800-373-2571

Promotes safe boating, seminars, poker run & jet ski races, carnival.

World Catfish Festival

Belzoni, Mississippi
April 5, 2003
www.catfishcapitalonline.com
662-247-4838

Fish fry, catfish eating contest, crowning the Catfish Queen, arts & crafts.

North Carolina

Autumn Leaves Festival

Mount Airy, North Carolina
October 10–12, 2003
www.visitmayberry.com
336-786-1005

Crafters, artists & vendors from six states, children's activities too.

Bele Chere

Asheville, North Carolina
July 25–27, 2003
www.belechere.com
828-259-5800

Street party charm entertains all of your senses, featuring music, crafts, activities.

Brushy Mountain Apple Festival

North Wilkesboro, North Carolina
October 4, 2003
www.applefestival.net
336-984-3022

Appalachian style demonstrations making molasses, apple butter & soap.

Cityfest Live!

Charlotte, North Carolina
April 25–27, 2003
www.cityfestlive.com
704.483.8555

Uptown's premier music event. Tickets on sale March 15, 2003.

CityStage ArtsFest

Greensboro, North Carolina
October 2–5, 2003
www.uacgreensboro.org
336-373-7523

Performing & visual arts, featuring local, regional & national performers.

CulloWHEE! ArtsFest

Featured on page 30
June 20–21, 2003
Cullowhee, North Carolina
www.cullowheeartsfest.com
828-227-7722

Jazz and blues music, national recording artists, local & regional musicians.

Eastern Music Festival

Greensboro, North Carolina
June 21 – July 26, 2003
www.easternmusicfestival.com
336-333-7450

Internationally-acclaimed classical music festival, professional concerts, training.

Fayetteville Dogwood Festival

Fayetteville, North Carolina
April 24–28, 2003
www.fayettevillenc.com/dogwood
910-323-1934

From sporting events to concerts, street dances to children's events.

Festival in the Park

Charlotte, North Carolina
September 18–21, 2003
www.festivalinthepark.org
704-338-1060

A wide range of visual arts & crafts, family-oriented entertainment.

Festival of Flowers

Asheville, North Carolina
April 5 – May 4, 2003
www.biltmore.com
800-624-1575

The Biltmore Estate showcases Victorian floral displays & garden paths.

Folkmoot USA

Waynesville, North Carolina
July 14–27, 2003
www.folkmoot.com
877-365-5872

International folk music & dance from renowned dance troupes.

Food Lion Speed Street

Charlotte, North Carolina
May 23–25, 2003
600festival.com
704-455-6814

Racing-related entertainment: interactive games, show cars, simulators.

Greenville Fine Art and Craft Festival

Greenville, North Carolina
October 10–12, 2003
kristisgallery.com
910-326-7222

New to Greenville, juried fine art & crafts presented by Kristi's Gallery.

Matthews Alive Festival

Matthews, North Carolina
August 29 – September 1, 2003
www.matthewsalive.org
704-849-3825

Music & children's entertainment with carnival games & arts & crafts.

Merlefest

Wilkesboro, North Carolina
April 24–27, 2003
www.merlefest.org
800-343-7857

Acoustic performers, instrument workshops, & vendors meet.

MumFest 2003

New Bern, North Carolina
October 10–12, 2003
www.mumfest.com
252-638-5781

Endless variety of attractions, including trolley rides & lumberjack show.

North Carolina Azalea Festival

Wilmington, North Carolina
April 2–4, 2003
www.ncazaleafestival.org
910-794-4650

Events include parade, street fair, celebrities, home & garden tours, concerts.

The Barbecue Festival

Lexington, North Carolina
October 25, 2003
www.barbecuefestival.com
336-956-1880

Pig themed sand sculpture, racing pigs, the Barbecue Carnival & Family Area.

Oklahoma

Aerospace America International Airshow

Oklahoma City, Oklahoma
June 13–15, 2003
www.aerospaceokc.com
405-685-9546

The hottest acts on the airshow circuit, civilian aerobatics pilots, aircraft displays.

Bank of Oklahoma–Williams Greenwood Jazz Celebration

Tulsa, Oklahoma
August 7–9, 2003
www.jazzongreenwood.com
918-584-3378

Cool jazz on warm summer nights, home of Oklahoma Jazz Hall of Fame.

Festival of the Arts

Oklahoma City, Oklahoma
April 22–27, 2003
www.artSouth
Carolinaouncilokc.com/festival
405-270-4848

Held outdoors on the grounds of the Myriad Gardens & Festival Plaza.

Norman Medieval Fair

Norman, Oklahoma
April 4–6, 2003
www.occe.ou.edu/medievalfair
405-288-2536

Jousting Knights, minstrels, human chess game, jugglers, magicians.

Red Earth Native American Cultural Festival

Oklahoma City, Oklahoma
May 23–25, 2003
www.redearth.org
405-427-5228

Native American tribes share the richness & diversity of their heritage.

Rooster Days Festival

Broken Arrow, Oklahoma
May 8–11, 2003
www.brokenarrow.org
918-251-1518

Rooster Days started in 1933, features parade, Miss Chick contest, carnival.

Sorghum Festival

Wewoka, Oklahoma
October 25, 2003
wwww.sorghum.org
405-257-5485

The autumn air is filled with the aroma and fun of this old-time fall tradition.

Tulsa Oktoberfest

Tulsa, Oklahoma
October 16–19, 2003
www.tulsaoktoberfest.org
918-744-9700

Folklife festival & Oktoberfest activities, bands from Germany, Austria, & U.S.

South Carolina

Charleston Rib Jam

Ladson, South Carolina
July 4–6, 2003
www.ribjam.com
843-626-5355

Friendly but fierce competition, $10,000 in prize money, bands each night.

3 Rivers Music Festival

Columbia, South Carolina
April 5–6, 2003
www.3riversmusicfestival.org
803.401.8990

Blues, jazz, rock, beach, gospel, hip-hop, country, unplugged & more.

Canadian American Days Festival

Myrtle Beach, South Carolina
March 8–16, 2003
seashell.myrtlebeachlive.com
843-626-7444 x7239

Concerts, dances, beach games, sports events greet spring-break vacationers.

Fall For Greenville

Greenville, South Carolina
October 10–12, 2003
www.greatergreenville.com
864-233-0461

Chili cook-off, cooking school, ice carving, bartender's mix-off, waiter's race.

Flowertown Festival

Summerville, South Carolina
April 4–6, 2003
www.summervilleymca.org/festival
843-871-9622

Two hundred fifty artists & craftsmen display their works.

Freedom Weekend Aloft

Anderson, South Carolina
May 23–26, 2003
www.freedomwkend.org
864-232-3700

Hot air balloons competing daily, national entertainers each evening.

South Carolina Festival of Roses

Orangeburg, South Carolina
April 25–27, 2003
www.festivalofroses.com
803-534-6821

Celebrate the rose season, tournaments, car show, arts & crafts.

Spoleto Festival USA

Charleston, South Carolina
May 23–June 8, 2003
www.spoletousa.org
843-722-2764

Opera, dance, theater, music in historic theaters, churches, & outdoor spaces.

Sun Fun Festival

Myrtle Beach, South Carolina
May 29–June 1, 2003
seashell.myrtlebeachlive.com
843-626-7444 x7239

Air show, beauty contests, sporting events, sandcastle-building contest.

The Pageland Watermelon Festival

Pageland, South Carolina
July 18–20, 2003
Budsftheart@shtc.net
843-672-6400

Watermelons & scrumptious food, magic acts, puppet shows, music.

Tennessee

Alhambra Shrine Fall Color Cruise and Folk Festival

Jasper, Tennessee
October 18–26, 2003
www.marioncountychamber.com
423-837-0747

Cruise in on the river & enjoy arts & crafts, children's activities, karaoke.

Celebrate Freedom!

Featured on page 34

August 9–23, 2003
Pigeon Forge, Tennessee
www.mypigeonforge.com
800-251-9100

Tribute to America's military veterans by musicals, forums, dances, performances.

Fan Fair

Nashville, Tennessee
June 5–8, 2003
www.fanfair.com
866-326-3247

Over 40 hours of Country Music concerts, autograph sessions, Family Zone.

Foothills Fall Festival

Maryville, Tennessee
October 10–12, 2003
www.ci.maryville.tn.us
865-981-1325

Downtown arts & crafts area, Adventure Land, carriage rides, petting zoo.

Fun Fest

Kingsport, Tennessee
July 18–26, 2003
www.funfest.net
423-392-8806

Community-oriented fun, music, 8K road race, concerts, hot air balloons.

Main Street Festival

Franklin, Tennessee
April 26–27, 2003
www.historicfranklin.com
615-595-1239

Arts & crafts, food, blues, pop, country, classical, rock music, carnival.

Memphis in May Beale Street Music Festival

Memphis, Tennessee
May 2–4, 2003
www.memphisinmay.org
901-525-4611

On the banks of the Mississippi River–blues, rock, gospel, R&B, alternative.

National Cornbread Festival

South Pittsburg, Tennessee
May 25–27, 2003
www.nationalcornbread.com
423-837-0022

All kinds of cornbread, cooking contest, 5K race, street dance, activities.

Riverbend Festival

Chattanooga, Tennessee
June 6–14, 2003
www.riverbendfestival.com
423-756-2212

National, regional & area music followed by a fantastic fireworks finale.

Smithville Fiddlers' Jamboree and Crafts Festival

Smithville, Tennessee
July 4–5, 2003
www.smithvilletn.com/jamboree
615-597-8500

Oldtime fiddle bands, clogging, buck dancing, dobro guitar, dulcimer, crafts.

Tennessee Walking Horse National Celebration

Shelbyville, Tennessee
August 20–30, 2003
www.twhnc.com
931-684-5915

The World's Greatest Horse Show–trade fair, southern cooking traditions.

Webb School Art and Craft Festival

Bell Buckle, Tennessee
October 18–19, 2003
www.thewebbschool.com
More than 800 exhibitors with an approximate crowd of 80,000 folks!

World Championship Barbecue Cooking Contest

Memphis, Tennessee
May 15–18, 2003
www.memphisinmay.org/barbecue
901-525-4611
Competitions: sauces, perfect ribs, shoulder, whole hog, "anything but".

Texas

Alliance Airport International Airshow

Fort Worth, Texas
October 11–12, 2003
www.allianceairshow.com
817-870-1515
Stunt flying, wing-walking & displays of military & civilian aircraft.

Amigo Airsho

El Paso, Texas
May 11–12, 2003
www.amigoairsho.org
915-532-5387
Civilian & military aircraft flying & on display, KidSho, WheelSho, TradeSho.

Art Splash on the Square

Graham, Texas
May 17, 2003
www.visitgraham.com
830-997-8515
Musicians, painters & performance artists entertain & demonstrate their crafts.

Bayfest

Corpus Christi, Texas
September 26–28, 2003
www.bayfesttexas.com
361-887-0868
Nationally recognized bands & artists country, tejano, Oldies, rock-n-roll.

Buccaneer Days

Corpus Christi, Texas
April 9 – May 4, 2003
www.bucdays.com
361-882-3242
City take-over for fun, parade, Blue Angels, rodeo, carnival, competitions.

Calle Espacial

Houston, Texas
March 14–16, 2003
www.callespacial.com
832-578-6394
The best in Latin & crossover music, food, family & fun.

Deep Ellum Arts Festival

Dallas, Texas
April 4–6, 2003
www.meifestivals.com
214-855-1881

A free-to-attend art party over six blocks of Downtown Dallas; bands, artists.

East Texas Yamboree

Gilmer, Texas
October 15–18, 2003
www.yamboree.com
903-843-2413

Tour de Yam, crowning Queen Yam & court, agricultural displays & contests.

Fiesta San Antonio

San Antonio, Texas
April 19–27, 2003
www.fiesta-sa.org
210-227-5191

Enjoy spicy music of diverse concerts & honor the heroes of the Alamo.

GrapeFest

Grapevine, Texas
September 11–14, 2003
www.grapevinetexasusa.com
817-410-3194

Sample award winning Texas wines & visit Grapevine's winery tasting rooms.

Houston International Festival

Houston, Texas
April 25 – May 4, 2003
www.ifest.org
800-541-2099

Diverse musical forms, regional, national & international performers, art.

International Festival Institute at Round Top

Featured on page 35

June 1 – July 12, 2003
Round Top, Texas
www.festivalhill.org
979-249-3129

Lecture & performance concert series with talented classical musicians.

Jazz'SAlive

San Antonio, Texas
September 20–21, 2003
www.saparksfoundation.org
210-212-8423

Top jazz entertainers, local talent, dinner/dance, Champagne Brunch.

Kaboom Town

Addison, Texas
July 3, 2003
www.addisontexas.net
800-752-6118

Fireworks are choreographed & simulcast, World-class Warbird flybys, games.

MAIN ST. Fort Worth Arts Festival

Fort Worth, Texas
April 24–27, 2003
www.msfwaf.org
817-336-2787

Fine artists, performance artists, music, dance, exhibitors, food vendors.

Mardi Gras of Southeast Texas

Port Arthur, Texas
February 27 – March 3, 2003
www.portarthur.com
409-721-8717

From arts & crafts to zydeco music & Parades, attractions for everyone.

Mayfest

Fort Worth, Texas
May 1–4, 2003
www.fortworth.com
817-332-1055

Art, local & major entertainment, sports, food, children's area with free activities.

Official Shrimporee of Texas

Aransas Pass, Texas
September 12–14, 2003
www.aransaspass.org
800-633-3028

Family entertainment & new ways to eat the tasty morsel, arts, races, contests.

Old Pecan Street Spring Arts Festival

Austin, Texas
May 3–4, 2003
www.roadstarproductions.com

25th Anniversary, an Austin tradition! Over 300 fine artists, music. Free.

Poteet Strawberry Festival

Poteet, Texas
April 10–13, 2003
www.strawberryfestival.com
830-742-8144

Concerts, specialty acts, thrill shows, children's area, rodeo, evening dances.

Rattlesnake Round-up

Sweetwater, Texas
March 7–9, 2003
www.rattlesnakeroundup.com
915-235-5488

Snake meat eating contest, guided snake hunts, awards for the most rattlesnakes.

Scarborough Renaissance Faire

Waxahachie, Texas
April 12–June 1, 2003
www.scarboroughrenfest.com
972-938-3247

The times of King Henry VIII, performers, hearty food, market.

Taste of Dallas in the West End

Dallas, Texas
July 11–13, 2003
www.tasteofdallas.org
214-741-7185

An extravaganza of food from fine restaurants, live music, vendors, activities.

Texas Folklife Festival

San Antonio, Texas
June 5–8, 2003
www.texasfolklifefestival.org
210-458-2390

Ethnic diversities on display with costumes, crafts, instruments & foods.

Texas Renaissance Festival

Plantersville, Texas
October 4 – November 16, 2003
www.texrenfest.com
800-458-3435

Gallant knights & lovely ladies recreate the romance of the Renaissance era.

Washington's Birthday Celebration

Laredo, Texas
February 8–23, 2003
www.wbcalaredo.org
956-722-0589

Celebrate cultures with Jalapeno Festival, parades, fireworks & carnival.

Wurstfest

New Braunfels, Texas
October 31 – November 9, 2003
wurstfest.com
800-221-4369

German culture & Texas fun, sample sausage & strudel, polka & waltz.

Virginia

Afr' Am Fest

Norfolk, Virginia
May 24–26, 2003
www.aframfest.com
757-456-1743

Arts & Culture celebration, marketplace, a fine art show, children's village.

AirPower Over Hampton Roads

Hampton, Virginia
June 21–22, 2003
www.langleyairshow.com
757-764-2018

AirPower after Dark, military & civilian acts, breathtaking aerial demonstrations.

Alexandria Red Cross Waterfront Festival

Alexandria, Virginia
June 6–8, 2003
www.waterfrontfestival.org
703-549-8300

Concerts, tall ships, fireworks, arts & crafts, children's events, refreshments.

Boardwalk Art Show and Festival

Virginia Beach, Virginia
June 12–15, 2003
www.cacv.org
757-425-0000

Juried arts show & performing arts against a backdrop of surf, sun & sand.

Celebrate Fairfax! 2003

Fairfax, Virginia
June 6–8, 2003
www.celebratefairfax.com
703-324-3247

Music, entertainment & tech festival, arts & crafts, quilt show, petting zoo.

Chincoteague Volunteer Firemen's Carnival

Chincoteague, Virginia
July 4 – August 2, 2003
www.chincoteaguechamber.com
757-336-6161

Rides, games, food, crafts, live entertainment, raffles, great family fun.

East Coast Surfing Championship and Music Festival

Virginia Beach, Virginia
August 21–25, 2003
www.surfecsc.com
757-491-6539

Pro & amateur surfing, volleyball, evening music all on a sandy beach.

Fall Festival

Fairfax, Virginia
October 11, 2003
ci.fairfax.va.us
703-385-7949

Streets full of juried crafts, pony rides, inflatable rides, family entertainment.

Fall Jubilee in Old Town Manassas

Manassas, Virginia
October 4, 2003
www.visitmanassas.org
703-361-6599

Community spirit & family fun with music, children's entertainment.

Historic Appomattox Railroad Festival

Appomattox, Virginia
October 11–12, 2003
www.appomattox.com
434-352-2338

Grand Parade, craft show, music, teddy bear parade, food, games.

Neptune Festival Airshow

Virginia Beach, Virginia
September 19–21, 2003
www.neptunefestival.com
757-427-3580 x889

Aerobatic demonstrations, grace, precision & power, exhibits, concerts.

Norfolk Harborfest

Norfolk, Virginia
June 6–8, 2003
www.norfolkharborfest.org
757-441-2345

View tall ships, character vessels & military craft, & party in the streets.

Norfolk's International Azalea Festival– A Salute to NATO

Norfolk, Virginia
April 21–27, 2003
www.azaleafestival.org
757-282-2801

Azaleas in bloom, parade of Nations, NATOFest, Queen dinner & ball.

Poquoson Seafood Festival

Poquoson, Virginia
October 17–19, 2003
www.seafestival.com
757-868-3588

Delicious food, arts & crafts, children's rides & games, fireworks.

Seawall Festival

Portsmouth, Virginia
June 6–8, 2003
www.portsevents.org

Family entertainment, children's area with jugglers, salt water touch tanks.

Second Street Festival

Richmond, Virginia
October 3–5, 2003
www.downtownpresents.org
804-788-6466

Jazz, gospel & big band music, The Marketplace & delicious food.

Shenandoah Valley Hot Air Balloon and Wine Festival

Millwood, Virginia
October 17–19, 2003
www.historiclongbranch.com
888-558-5567

Hot air balloons & powered parachutes, specialty shops, Virginia wine tasting.

SunCom Bayou Boogaloo and Cajun Food Festival

Norfolk, Virginia
June 20–22, 2003
www.bayouboogaloo.org
757-441-2345

Spicy weekend on the waterfront. Funky zydeco music & Cajun delicacies.

SunCom Jazz Norfolk Concert in Town Point Park

Norfolk, Virginia
August 16, 2003
www.festeventsva.org/festevents
757-441-2345

Sizzling jazz by well-known regional & national entertainers on the waterfront.

SunCom Virginia Children's Festival

Norfolk, Virginia
October 4, 2003
www.childrensfest.org
757-441-2345

A whole day full of activities geared toward children.

Urbanna Oyster Festival

Urbanna, Virginia
October 31 – November 1, 2003
www.urbannaoysterfestival.com
804-758-0368

Oysters, food of all types, entertainment & activities on the waterfront.

Virginia Arts Festival

Norfolk, Virginia
April 25 – May 25, 2003
www.virginiaartsfest.com
800-386-4682 or 757-282-2822

A spectacle of pageantry & music, multiple music genres, drama.

Virginia Highlands Festival

Abingdon, Virginia
July 26 – August 10, 2003
www.vahighlandsfestival.org
540-676-2282

Juried arts show & antique market, celebrates area culture & history.

Virginia International Tattoo

Norfolk, Virginia
April 25–27, 2003
www.virginiaartsfest.com
757-282-2822

Pageantry, ceremony, marching bands, drill teams, choral groups.

Virginia Lake Festival

Clarksville, Virginia
July 18–20, 2003
www.kerrlake.com/chamber
804-374-2436

Juried arts & crafts, hot air balloons, antique cars, Gathering of the Boats.

West Virginia

Charleston Sternwheel Regatta Festival

Charleston, West Virginia
August 28 – September 1, 2003
www.sternwheelregatta.com
304-348-6419

River event with races, A Taste of Charleston, parades, fireworks, concerts.

New River Gorge Bridge Day Festival

Fayetteville, West Virginia
October 17–18, 2003
www.newrivercvb.com
304-465-5617

The world's longest single arch steel span bridge open to pedestrians, activities.

West Virginia Black Walnut Festival

Spencer, West Virginia
October 9–12, 2003
www.wvblackwalnutfestival.org
304-927-1780

Celebrates the walnut harvest in Roane County, parades, crafts, concerts.

West Virginia Italian Heritage Festival

Clarksburg, West Virginia
August 29–31, 2003
www.wvihf.com
304-622-7314

Color, pageantry, entertainment, contests, exhibitions & displays.

Washington D.C.

International ChildArt Festival

Washington, D.C.
September 6–13, 2003
www.icaf.org/202-530-1000

Premier international event for children, hosts national child artists of the world.

Safeway's National Capital Barbecue Battle

Washington, D.C.
June 21–22, 2003
www.barbecuebattle.com
202-828-3099

Barbecue championship battle, sampling pavilion, fantastic entertainment.

National Cherry Blossom Festival

Washington, D.C.
March 22 – April 7, 2003
www.nationalcherryblossomfestival.org
202-547-1500

Springtime glory of Japanese cherry trees in bloom, sporting events, parade.

Smithsonian Folklife Festival

Washington, D.C.
June 25 – July 6, 2003
www.folklife.si.edu
202-287-3424

Each year, the Festival hosts special programs on a geographic region or point.

Connecticut

Meet the Artists and Artisans Spring Show

Milford, Connecticut
May 17–18, 2003
www.meettheartistsandartisans.com
203-874-5672

Outdoor green show with juried exhibits in the historic center of town.

Apple Harvest Festival

Southington, Connecticut
October 4–12, 2003
www.appleharvestfestival.com
860-628-8036

Parade, carnival, arts & crafts, road races, live entertainment & plenty of food.

Boats, Books, and Brushes

New London, Connecticut
September 5–7, 2003
www.sailnewlondon.com
860-443-8332

Unique maritime event, literature, arts, food, authors' readings, book signings.

Glastonbury Apple Harvest Festival

Glastonbury, Connecticut
October 18–19, 2003
www.glastonburychamber.org
860-659-3587

Rides & games, music, clowns, crafts, contests, great food, parade.

Greater Hartford Festival of Jazz

Hartford, Connecticut
July 18–20, 2003
www.jazzhartford.org
860-872-5485

Bushnell Park features international as well as local talent. Free.

Hartford's Mark Twain Days

Hartford, Connecticut
August 29 – September 1, 2003
www.riverfront.org

Civil war reenactments, medieval jousting, fireworks & headliner entertainment.

International Festival of Arts and Ideas

New Haven, Connecticut
June 13–28, 2003
www.artidea.org
888-278-4332

A 16-day celebration of the arts.

Meriden Daffodil Festival

Meriden, Connecticut
April 26–27, 2003
www.daffodilfest.com
203-630-4259

Antique Show, Little Miss Daffodil, Daffodils on Parade, games, exhibits.

Mystic Outdoor Art Festival

Mystic, Connecticut
August 9–10, 2003
lauren@mysticchamber.org
860-572-5098

Artists & craftsmen display & sell, live entertainment, Future Artists Pavilion.

New Haven Jazz Festival

New Haven, Connecticut
August 9–23, 2003
www.newhavenjazz.com
203-946-7821

Annual free jazz concert series includes concerts on the New Haven Green.

Norfolk Chamber Music Festival

Norfolk, Connecticut
June 22 – August 17, 2003
www.yale.edu/norfolk
860-542-3000

National & international performers, ensembles, workshops, forums, lectures.

Oyster Festival

Norwalk, Connecticut
September 5–7, 2003
www.seaport.org
203-838-9444

Oyster Slurping & Shucking, maritime & oyster exhibits, Vintage Vessels.

Plainville Fire Company Hot Air Balloon Festival

Plainville, Connecticut
August 22–24, 2003
www.plainvilleballoonfestival.com
860-747-2521

Morning & evening balloon flights, weather permitting.

Red Hot Blues and Chili Cookoff

East Hartford, Connecticut
July 26–27, 2003
kpreston@modimes.org
860-290-5440

Area firehouses compete with their best chili, blues b& competition.

Riverfest

Hartford, Connecticut
July 5, 2003
www.riverfront.org
860-713-3131

Join the fun! Fireworks, live entertainment, vendors, children's activities.

Sailfest

New London, Connecticut
July 11–13, 2003
www.sailfest.org
860-444-1879

Street & harbor festival, Tall Ships, amusement rides, crafts, fireworks.

SoNo Arts Celebration

South Norwalk, Connecticut
August 2–3, 2003
www.sonoarts.org
203-866-7916

Supports various forms of art & performances, promotes community spirit.

Subfest

Groton, Connecticut
July 3–6, 2003
mwr.subasenlon.navy.mil
860-694 3238

Animal acts & attractions, wild west show, carnival, rides, marketplace.

Taste of Connecticut Food Festival

Mystic, Connecticut
September 5–7, 2003
www.mystic.ct.us/taste
860-536-3575

Restaurants serve appetizer-sized portions of their best dishes; entertainment.

Taste of Hartford

Hartford, Connecticut
June 11–15, 2003
www.tasteofhartford.com
860-920-5337

Enjoy every kind of cuisine, continuous entertainment & festivities.

Maine

La Kermesse Festival

Biddeford, Maine
June 26–29, 2003
la_kermesse_crafts@hotmail.com
207-468-6952

Fireworks kick-off, parade, a weekend of entertainment & rides.

National Folk Festival

Bangor, Maine
August 22–24, 2003
www.nationalfolkfestival.com
1-800-91-MOOSE

Brings together the very best traditional performers from around the world.

Yarmouth Clam Festival

Yarmouth, Maine
July 18–20, 2003
www.clamfestival.com
207-846-3984

Food Circle–seafood delicacies & other delights–musicians, humorists, dancers.

Massachusetts

Boston Harborfest

Boston, Massachusetts
July 1–6, 2003
www.bostonharborfest.com
617-227-1528

Celebrate colonial & maritime history, fireworks, reenactments, tours, concerts.

Cambridge River Festival

Boston, Massachusetts
June 14, 2003
www.ci.cambridge.ma.us
617-349-4380
Local & regional performing groups, individual artists, & arts organizations.

Jacob's Pillow Dance Festival

Becket, Masachusetts
June 18 – August 24, 2003
www.jacobspillow.org
413-243-0745
Offers a School, Archives, free events, live music, world premieres.

Lowell Folk Festival

Lowell, Massachusetts
July 25–27, 2003
www.lowellfolkfestival.org
978-970-5000
Traditional music & dance, craft demonstrations, ethnic foods, activities.

Peter Pan Taste of Springfield

Springfield, Massachusetts
June 11–14, 2003
www.spiritofspringfield.org
413-733-3800
Outdoor food court, eateries sell sample portions of their specialties.

Revere Beach Seafood Festival

Featured on page 19
Revere, Massachusetts
August 16–17, 2003
www.rbsff.com
508.788.0333
Beach party! Music, performers, restaurants serving signature seafood dishes.

San Antonio Di Padova Da Montefalcione

Boston, Massachusetts
August 29–31, 2003
www.stanthonysfeast.com
617-723-8669
Largest Italian Religious Festival in New England, food, parades, games.

Tanglewood Jazz Festival

Lenox, Massachusetts
August 29 – September 1, 2003
www.bso.org
800-274-8499
A great jazz music festival on 210-acre estate in the Berkshire Mountains.

Whaling City Festival

New Bedford, Massachusetts
July 11–13, 2003
whalingcityfestival.com
508-996-3348
Rides, carnival, craft & flea markets, custom car, truck & motorcycle show.

Westminster Fallfest 2003

Westminster, Massachusetts
September 25–28, 2003
www.westminsterfallfest.com
410-848-9393

Parade, food, games, live entertainment, contests, Scarecrow making, karaoke.

New Hampshire

Frostbite Follies Winter Carnival

Littleton, New Hampshire
February 7–9, 2003
www.littletonareachamber.com
603-444-6561

Ice sculptures, historic hotel tours, snowmobile events, dances, sleigh rides.

Hampton Beach Seafood Festival

Hampton Beach, New Hampshire
September 5–7, 2003
www.hamptonbeach.org
603-926-8717

Entertainment enlivens the selection of seafood specialties, most under $5.

Highland Games at Loon Mountain

Contoocook, New Hampshire
September 19–21, 2003
www.nhscot.org
603-229-1975

Gathering of the Clans, Highland Dance, seminars, workshops.

Keene Pumpkin Festival

Keene, New Hampshire
October 24–25, 2003
www.centerstagenh.com
603-358-5344

Towers of pumpkins, downtown brimming with lit jacks–pumpkins galore!

Somersworth International Children's Festival

Somersworth, New Hampshire
June 21, 2003
www.nhfestivals.org
603-692-5869

International entertainment, exhibits, foods, children's activities.

New Jersey

Academy of Music Summer Festival

Featured on page 24

Mahwah, New Jersey
June 30 – August 3, 2003
aomfestival@cs.com
845-357-5459

Instrumental & chamber music study, performances, master classes.

Bloomfield Harvest Fest

Bloomfield, New Jersey
September 20–21, 2003
Bloomfieldharvestfest.home.att.net
973-680-4189

A big block party–continuous entertainment, ethnic foods & kids' area.

Wheels & Wings Airshow

Millville, New Jersey
May 3–4, 2003
www.schultzairshows.com
856-327-2347

Airshow & car show, flying each day, over 100 aircraft on display.

Cruisin' with the Oldies

Red Bank, New Jersey
May 16–18, 2003
www.innatelygoodtimes.com
732-747-7728

Features an antique & classic car show, nostalgic music, exhibits & a carnival.

Hoboken Fall Arts and Music Festival

Hoboken, New Jersey
September 21, 2003
www.nj.com/hobokenfest
201-420-2207

Over 250 artists, crafters, sculptors & photographers, special children's area.

Hoboken Italian Festival

Hoboken, New Jersey
September 4–7, 2003
www.madonnahoboken.com
201-653-2699

Waterfront extravaganza emulates the Feast of the Madonna Dei Martiti.

Hoboken Spring Arts & Music Festival

Hoboken, New Jersey
May 4, 2003
www.nj.com/hobokenfest
201-420-2388

Artists, crafters & photographers, an eclectic mix of local music & food.

Mercer County Italian American Festival

West Windsor, New Jersey
September 19–21, 2003
www.italianamericanfestival.com
609-631-7544

Cultural exhibits & vendors, entertainment, presentations. Free.

Quick Chek New Jersey Festival of Ballooning

Readington, New Jersey
July 25–27, 2003
www.balloonfestival.com
800-468-2479

Celebrate the magic of hot air ballooning, ascensions twice daily.

Red Bank Jazz and Blues Festival

Red Bank, New Jersey
May 30 – June 1, 2003
www.Redbankfestival.com
732-899-3262

Local, regional & national jazz & blues performances set in a park on the river.

Saint Gregory The Great Carnival

Trenton, New Jersey
June 16–21, 2003
609-587-4877

Fun, great rides by Amusements of America & lots of entertainment.

Shad Fest

Lambertville, New Jersey
April 26–27, 2003
www.newhopepa.com/
Lambertville
201-653-2699

Mad about Shad! Residents sing about it, draw it, look at it, catch it, & eat it.

New York

Albany Tulip Festival

Albany, New York
May 9–11, 2003
www.albanyevents.org/
tulip_festival
518-434-2032

Tulip show, the old world tradition of scrubbing the streets, Kinderkermis.

Allentown Art Festival

Buffalo, New York
June 14–15, 2003
www.allentownartfestival.org
716-881-4269

Artists & crafters from the U.S. & Canada gather in historic district.

Canal Fest

North Tonawanda, New York
July 13–20, 2003
www.canalfest.org
716-692-3292

Community celebration featuring a wide variety of activities for the family.

Celebrate Brooklyn! Performing Arts Festival

Brooklyn, New York
June 12 – August 15, 2003
www.celebratebrooklyn.org
718-855-7882

Brooklyn Information & Culture program of music, dance, film.

Chenango Summer MusicFest

Featured on page 26

June 19–22, 2003
Hamilton, New York
groups.colgate.edu/musicfest
315-228-7642

a special blend of chamber music festivities & education with daily themes.

Corn Hill Arts Festival

Rochester, New York
July 12–13, 2003
www.cornhill.org
585-262-3142

A celebration of city living with a commitment to the arts.

Fall Foliage Festival

Cohocton, New York
October 3–5, 2003
corningfingerlakes.com
607-936-6544

Check out the crafts, parades, music, soccer tournament, tree-sitting contest.

Finger Lakes Wine Festival

Featured on page 27

Watkins Glen, New York
July 18–20, 2003
www.flwinefest.com
607-535-2481

Wineries offer tastings, seminars & demonstrations, music, arts & crafts.

Greenwich Village Halloween Parade

New York, New York
October 31, 2003
www.halloween-nyc.com
212-475-3333 x4044

Costumed marchers, specially commissioned puppets, marching bands.

Grey Fox Bluegrass Festival

Featured on page 28

Ancramdale, New York
July 17–20, 2003
www.greyfoxbluegrass.com
888-946-8495

Bluegrass on the Rothvoss Farm, dance pavilion & instruction, workshops.

Harborfest

Oswego, New York
July 24–27, 2003
oswegoharborfest.com
315-343-3373

Family reunion atmosphere, music, children's parade, arts & crafts, fireworks.

Hilton Apple Fest

Hilton, New York
October 4–5, 2003
www.hiltonapplefest.org
585-392-7773

Quality entertainment & delicious apple creations, Apple Fest Lore & Legend.

Lilac Festival

Rochester, New York
May 9–18, 2003
www.lilacfestival.com
716-256-4960

Lilacs in bloom at Highland Park (park designer Frederick Law Olmstead).

Lincoln Center Festival

New York, New York
July 7–27, 2003
www.lincolncenter.org
212-875-5928

Multicultural celebration, music, theater & dance; new works, revivals.

Macy's Thanksgiving Day Parade

New York, New York
November 27, 2003
www.macyparade.com
212-494-4495

Macy's Parade is Thanksgiving, isn't it?

New York Film Festival

New York, New York
September 26 – October 12, 2003
www.filmlinc.com/nyff
212 875-5610

Newest & most important cinematic works from around the world.

New York Renaissance Faire

Tuxedo, New York
August 2 – September 14, 2003
www.renfair.com/NY
845-351-5174

Bustling recreation of a 16th Century marketplace with costumed characters.

New York State Festival of Balloons

Dansville, New York
August 29 – September 1, 2003
www.nysfob.com
716-335-8885

Early morning flights & mass evening launches thrill the crowds.

Park Avenue Summer Art Fest

Rochester, New York
August 2–3, 2003
www.rochesterevents.com
585-473-4482

A juried art & craft sale, musical performances & unique shopping.

San Gennaro Feast and Street Fair

New York, New York
September 11–21, 2003
www.littleitalynyc.com
212-768-932

The most popular feature of this Little Italy festival is the sausage sandwiches!

Saratoga Festival and Dressage

Featured on page 29

Saratoga Springs, New York
May 24–26, 2003
www.saratogaarcfestival.org
518-587-0723
Dressage, precision riding, pageantry, International exotic all-breed show.

Sterling Renaissance Festival and Summer Market Place

Sterling, New York
July 5 – August 17, 2003
Queen Elizabeth & her entourage of lords & ladies come to life.

Syracuse Jazz Fest

Syracuse, New York
June 21–23, 2003
www.syracusejazzfest.com
315-422-8284
Legendary masters demonstrate past jazz, up-&-comers are the future of jazz.

Taste of Buffalo

Buffalo, New York
July 12–13, 2003
www.tasteofbuffalo.com
716-831-9376
One of the largest food & entertainment extravaganzas in the nation.

WNED Buffalo Niagara Guitar Festival

Buffalo, New York
June 14–21, 2003
www.buffaloniagaraguitarfestival.com
716-845-7156
Top-notch performances as well as guitar competitions & workshops.

Pennsylvania

Allegheny County Coors Light Rib Cook-Off

Pittsburgh, Pennsylvania
August 29 – September 1, 2003
www.theribcookoff.com
412-678-1727
Family fun, musical entertainment & sizzling ribs smoked to perfection.

Apple Harvest Festival

Gettysburg, Pennsylvania
October 4–12, 2003
www.gettysburg.com
717-334-6274
Savor apple products–jellies, syrups, cider, butter, desserts–orchard tours.

Celtic Classic

Bethlehem, Pennsylvania
September 26–28, 2003
www.celticfest.org
610-868-9599
Experience Ireland, Scotland, & Wales–Highland music, athletics, dance.

Central Pennsylvania Festival of the Arts

State College, Pennsylvania
July 9–13, 2003
arts-festival.com
814-237-3682

Celebration of visual & performing arts, juried, outdoor fine arts & crafts show.

Christkindlmarkt

Bethlehem, Pennsylvania
November 28 – December 21, 2003
www.christkindlmarkt.org
610-861-0678

Heated tents house fine craftsmen & artists displaying & selling goods.

Fort Ligonier Days

Ligonier, Pennsylvania
October 10–12, 2003
www.ligonier.com
724-238-4200

The Battle of Fort Ligonier re-enacted with artillery demonstrations.

Funfest Weekend

Hazleton, Pennsylvania
September 6–7, 2003
www.hazletonchamber.org
800-OKF-FEST

Craft show, street fair, muscle cars, parade, fireworks, free entertainment.

Gettysburg Civil War Heritage Days

Gettysburg, Pennsylvania
June 27 – July 6, 2003
www.gettysburgcvb.org
717-334-6274

Living history re-enacted: army campsites & battles, with lectures, concerts.

Gettysburg: Three Days of Destiny 140th Anniversary Battle

Gettysburg, Pennsylvania
July 4–6, 2003
www.gettysburgreenactment.com
717-338-1525

Take advantage of opportunity to visit with gifted & talented living historians.

Johnstown FolkFest

Johnstown, Pennsylvania
August 29–31, 2003
www.jaha.org
888-222-1889

Traditional music & ethnic foods in a historical working-class neighborhood.

Kutztown Festival

Kutztown, Pennsylvania
June 28 – July 6, 2003
kutztownfestival.com
888-674-6136

Portays aspects of Pennsylvania Dutch life from the 18th & 19th century.

Mayfair Festival of the Arts

Allentown, Pennsylvania
May 22–26, 2003
www.mayfairfestival.org
610-437-6900

Over 250 free performances, programs, & events.

Musikfest

Bethlehem, Pennsylvania
August 1–10, 2003
www.musikfest.org
610-861-0678

Satisfy your musical tastes with over a thousand free, live performances.

NAS JRB Willow Grove AIR FEST

Willow Grove, Pennsylvania
September 13–14, 2003

Civilian & military flying acts, demonstrations, aircraft displays, activities.

Pennsylvania Renaissance Faire

Manheim, Pennsylvania
August 16 – October 26, 2003
www.parenaissancefaire.com
717-665-7021

A colorfully costumed cast of hundreds in Merrie Olde England. Weekends.

Pittsburgh International Children's Festival

Pittsburgh, Pennsylvania
May 14–18, 2003

Kids can explore the world through theater, music, dance, circus & puppetry.

Pittsburgh Three Rivers Regatta

Pittsburgh, Pennsylvania
August 7–10, 2003
www.pghregatta.com
412-875-2153

Largest inland regatta in the country–Regatta Grand Prix & Regatta Thunder.

Shadyside Arts Festival

Pittsburgh, Pennsylvania
August 8–10, 2003
www.shadysideartsfestival.com
412-621-8481

Fine arts & crafts, interactive areas, artist demonstrations, music, dance.

Sunoco Welcome America! Festival

Philadelphia, Pennsylvania
June 27 – July 6, 2003
phila.gov/Sunoco
215-683-2208

Celebrate the nation's birthday & the cultures woven inro our history.

Three Rivers Arts Festival

Pittsburgh, Pennsylvania
June 6–22, 2003
www.artsfestival.net
412-281-8723
Juried visual arts exhibits, artists' market, music, children's activities.

Westmoreland Arts and Heritage Festival

Greensburg, Pennsylvania
July 4–7, 2003
www.artsandheritage.com
724-834-7474
Two national fine art exhibits, Civil War & Indian encampments, performances.

Rhode Island

Convergence International Arts Festival

Providence, Rhode Island
September 5–21, 2003
www.caparts.org
401-621-1992
Over 30 sculpture installations, live music, dance & theatre performances.

Gaspee Days

Warwick, Rhode Island
May 3 – June 8, 2003
www.gaspee.com
401-781-1772
Arts & crafts contests, parade, reenactments emphasizin on colonial militias.

Newport Music Festival

Newport, Rhode Island
July 11–27, 2003
www.newportmusic.org
401-846-1133
Summer mansions showcase classical concerts in ballrooms & on lawns.

Newport Waterfront Irish Festival

Newport, Rhode Island
August 30 – September 1, 2003
www.newportfestivals.com/Irish_Festival
401-846-1600
Authentic Irish Festival entertainment, step dancing hall, crafts, cuisine.

Rhythm & Roots

Featured on page 32
August 29–31, 2003
Charlestown, Rhode Island
www.rhythmandroots.com
888-855-6940
Southern roots music, dance and food festival, lessons, workshops, activities.

Schweppes Great Chowder Cook-Off

Featured on page 33
June 7, 2003
Newport, Rhode Island
www.newportfestivals.com
401-846-1600
Hot competition for best clam, seafood or creative chowder; music & demos.

Vermont

Discover Jazz Festival

Burlington, Vermont
June 2–8, 2003
www.discoverjazz.com
802-863-7992
Concerts, dances, jams, workshops, jazz, blues, funk, gospel, swing, zydeco.

Vermont Maple Festival

St. Albans, Vermont
April 25–27, 2003
www.vtmaplefestival.org
802-524-5800
Famous maple syrup sugared on snow, on pancakes, & with other tasty treats.